Formulators
OF THE
FORMULA of CONCORD

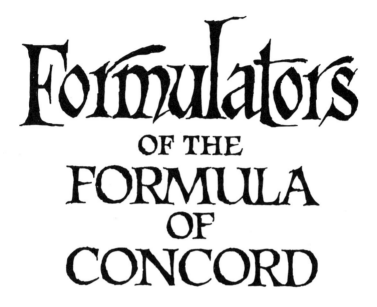

Formulators
OF THE
FORMULA
OF
CONCORD

Four Architects
of Lutheran Unity

❦

THEODORE R. JUNGKUNTZ

Publishing House
St. Louis

Concordia Publishing House, St. Louis, Missouri
Copyright © 1977 Concordia Publishing House
MANUFACTURED IN THE UNITED STATES OF AMERICA

Library of Congress Cataloging in Publication Data

Jungkuntz, Theodore R 1932-
    The formulators of the Formula of concord.

    Bibliography: p.
    1. Andreae, Jakob, 1528-1590. 2. Chemnitz, Martin, 1522-1586. 3. Selnecker, Nikolaus, 1530-1592. 4. Chytraeus, David, 1531-1600. 5. Lutheran Church—Biography. 6. Lutheran Church. Formula of concord. I. Title. BX8079.J86   230'.4'10922 [B]   76-40948
ISBN 0-570-03740-9

To Lois

CONTENTS

PREFACE

Providence is stranger than fiction. The initial invitation to write a book under the title *The Formulators of the Formula of Concord* came in September 1965. At that time it was projected as one of a series to be entitled "Profiles in Lutheranism." The goal was a manuscript from me by July 1966 in order to launch the series in 1967—the 450th anniversary of the Ninety-five Theses. Reverse the last two digits of 1967 and we have the date of this writing, 1976. The "Profiles" series was scuttled before it was launched, but little by little, year by year, the present volume took shape, and with it we now hope to launch the celebration of the 400th anniversary of the writing of the Formula of Concord.

A special expression of God's providential guidance I recognize in my being appointed as director of Valparaiso University's foreign study center, located in Reutlingen, Germany, for the years 1969—72. From this location I had easy access to libraries located in Tuebingen and Stuttgart, and through the efforts of a helpful friend, Louis Reith, obtained from these institutions a great volume of Xeroxed materials essential to the research for this study.

A second expression of God's providence came by way of a sabbatical semester granted me in the fall of 1973 by Valparaiso University, only one year after my three-year absence from the home campus. This period of time afforded me my longest uninterrupted absence from the classroom and thus an opportunity to get the bulk of the work done.

But only that can be completed which is first of all begun, and for the invitation to begin my thanks go to Hank Kadai of Concordia Seminary, Springfield, Ill. In that invitation I recognize the surprising providence of God. And for the encouragement to pursue what I had begun I thank Arthur Carl Piepkorn, now of blessed memory, the man who I wish could have written the book under this title.

Finally, only that can be published which is first of all typed, and for this arduous task I thank my faithful wife, Lois, and my children, Becky and Teddy, who lovingly curtailed their demands on their mother so as to allow her time for this sacrifice of love.

What began by God's providence and what was attended by His providence to its completion, I now commend to His continuing providence, desiring only that it prove to be a blessing to a church once again seeking *concordia*. May our celebration in 1977, God willing, of a *concordia* initially observed in 1577 be the occasion for a new release of that Spirit which Jesus once breathed on His disciples and which He instructs us to share with one another (John 20:19-23).
Theodore Jungkuntz

June 25, 1976
446th Anniversary of the Presentation of the Augsburg Confession
Valparaiso, Ind.

INTRODUCTION

Some Lutheran church bodies today look with pride upon the fact that they are committed to "believe, teach, and confess" in keeping with the Formula of Concord, a confession completed in 1577 and first published as part of *The Book of Concord* in 1580. Other Lutheran churches pride themselves that their confessional commitment stops short of the Formula. Reflected in this difference is the priority which a church body gives to reading a confession either as a historically conditioned document or as a work of the Holy Spirit.[1] Those who emphasize the suprahistorical dimension of Christian confessions tend also to be more highly appreciative of the Formula than those who feel compelled to emphasize the historical conditionedness of such confessions. In our present study of the lives of the four chief formulators of the Formula of Concord it is our intention to permit the historical factors leading to the framing of this document to come to as full an expression as the limits imposed upon us permit. But this is done not with the aim of detracting from the abiding spiritual and metahistorically initiated authority of this confession but rather to enable us all the more clearly to discover *that* in the Formula of Concord which alone can make it authoritative in the church today—*the prophetic and apostolic Gospel of Jesus Christ.*[2]

Although a number of political rulers—especially Duke Christoph of Wuerttemberg (and his son and successor in 1568, Ludwig), Duke Julius of Braunschweig, Landgrave William of Hesse, and Elector August of Saxony—were shakers and movers when it came to providing impetus, means, and direction to the formulation of the Formula of Concord, their impact came to final expression only through their appointed theologians. Consequently their significance will be sufficiently recognized if in the appropriate place we make ourselves aware of the influence they had on the theologians ultimately responsible for authoring the Formula.

It is also generally acknowledged that six men were intimately involved in the final stages of writing and editing what became the

Formula of Concord at Torgau in 1576 and Bergen Abbey in 1577, but two of these men, Andrew Musculus and Christopher Koerner, played such a minor role (their presence and participation having had church-political significance rather than decisively affecting the written formulation of the document)[3] that their omission from this study will not significantly detract from its value in terms of our stated purpose and aim.

That leaves us with the four men who were almost exclusively responsible for the wording of the Formula of Concord—Jakob Andreae, Martin Chemnitz, David Chytraeus, and Nikolaus Selnecker. By taking a close look at the lives of these men, especially at their activities as they culminated in the formulation of the Formula of Concord, the distinct historical causes and effects leading to the Formula should enter our consciousness and help us to make the difficult but necessary distinction between that in the Formula of Concord which has abiding and binding validity and that which has only limited, temporal, and relative significance. This exercise both in detecting the relationship between historical conditions and confessional formulations and in distinguishing the earthen vessel from the enduring treasure could very well serve Christians today as they together struggle to confess the old faith in terms meaningful in the present crisis of Christianity.

The Formula of Concord also came into existence at the occasion of a crisis in Christianity. At stake was the Gospel that had found articulation in the theology of Martin Luther, particularly as expressed in the Augsburg Confession of 1530, written by Luther's colleague, companion, and co-worker, Philip Melanchthon, and in Luther's own distillations of his theology, his Large and Small Catechisms of 1529 and his Smalcald Articles of 1537. The crisis was occasioned when, shortly after Luther's death (1546) and the military catastrophe of German Protestantism signaled by the victory of Charles V at Muehlberg (1547), the Augsburg and Leipzig Interims were promulgated as law (1548). These documents represented compromise efforts by Emperor Charles V to settle temporarily the religious controversy between the Roman Catholics and the Evangelicals. Intended as temporary solutions only, it was anticipated that the definitive solution would be effected by the Council of Trent, which had begun its sessions in 1545.

But neither the Interims nor the Council of Trent brought the desired peace. Whereas the latter was too forthright in its condemnation of Lutheran doctrine, the former were too obviously compromise

12

formulations heavily biased in favor of the Roman Catholic position, especially with reference to the celebration of the Mass and its accompanying ceremonial. Melanchthon, apprehensive about the chances of survival for the Evangelical faith, felt himself compelled to compromise evangelical freedom by yielding to Roman Catholic demands in matters of ritual in exchange for a moderately stated Lutheran doctrine of justification. Although he later admitted his error, he was never able to free himself from the stigma which attached to this show of weakness. The ensuing struggle between his followers and those of the hyper-Lutheran Matthias Flacius is usually referred to as the "adiaphoristic controversy," and it remained an issue until the time of the Formula of Concord, especially since it raised the question as to whether the course which had been suggested by the Interims should be specifically condemned in new confessional formulations. It was a crisis in the understanding of the Gospel since it involved the freedom which attached to this Gospel.

There were also other theological controversies soon in evidence. One group clustered around facets of the doctrine of justification—the Majoristic, the antinomistic, the synergistic, and the Osiandrian controversies—and another group around the Christological basis of justification, especially as this came to expression in the Crypto-Calvinistic controversies.[4] But in every instance it was the Gospel as it had been confessed in the Augsburg Confession of 1530 which was in dispute.

Nevertheless it would be an oversimplification of church history and an abstraction of the church from history if one were to think that the motives behind the doctrinal controversies were purely theological and reflected concern for nothing else than the articulation of Christian doctrine in truth and purity. Apart from the vested interests and mixed motives shaping and directing each of the four chief formulators of the Formula of Concord, one must keep in view the entire larger stage on which the action takes place with its social, cultural, political, and theological settings. Throughout the history of the church there is evidence that conflicting theological positions have served not only the clarification of Christian truth but also the identification of conflicting social, cultural, and political types.[5] This being the case, it is necessary that we here briefly indicate the nature of the most important of these conflicts in reference to the eventual formulation of the Formula of Concord.

Historians commonly distinguish between three theological parties involved in the disputes finally clarified by the Formula:

1) *The Philippists.* These were the followers of Philip Melanchthon, who thought of their master, with his seemingly more flexible theological positions, as the most reliable and authoritative interpreter and adapter of Luther for the critical times arising after Luther's death. Most of the doctrines eventually rejected by the Formula of Concord were maintained and defended by this group.

2) *The Gnesio-Lutherans.* So-called because they thought of themselves as those disciples of Luther who followed their master most strictly, they were represented particularly by men like Matthias Flacius (1520—75) and Nikolaus von Amsdorf (1483—1565). They were prepared to oppose the Philippists even at the risk of their own lives, and they made the condemnation of heretics a key issue of the ongoing debate. However, Flacius left himself open to precisely such a condemnation by his assertion that original sin is not an "accident" but the very "substance" of fallen man,[6] and Amsdorf did the same by his teaching that good works are detrimental to salvation.[7]

3) *The Center-Party.* Whereas the other two parties were clearly defined from the outset of the controversies, this Center-Party came into being as a direct result of the entire process of pacification conducted by those loyal Lutherans who could not feel comfortable with either of the above extremes. All of the formulators of the Formula of Concord would fall into this group.

It is now of interest to ask which factors, other than the purely theological, may have contributed to the formation of these three constellations of theologians.

One factor which ought to be kept in mind is the ongoing rivalry that existed between the two Saxon houses—Ernestine Saxony, which held the electorate until 1547, and Albertine Saxony, which succeeded to the electorate after that date. To be in possession of the electoral privilege was no small honor, so it is not surprising that when one house lost the honor to the other, considerable political hostility ensued. Precisely this occurred in this instance as a result of the conniving Duke Maurice, who by his support of Charles V had wrenched the electoral title to himself and the Albertine house. Thereby the region about Wittenberg, known as the "electoral circle," also fell to Albertine Saxony. This meant that Wittenberg University, dominated by Melanchthon, was now under Albertine jurisdiction. Whereas the Philippists adjusted to the change, the Gnesio-Lutherans relocated at the University of Jena, the school Ernestine Saxony substituted for its loss of Wittenberg. So the theological differences continued, but now the flames were also fed by those gathering tinder for the collaborationists on the one hand and for the resistance on the other.[8] Similarly Leipzig supported Wittenberg whereas Magdeburg supported Jena.

Certainly the master key for opening the doors of the political antechambers leading into the theological auditorium of the Formula of Concord is the Peace of Augsburg of 1555. The terms of the Peace were such that adherents of the Augsburg Confession were to enjoy the toleration granted by the principle that "he who owns the land determines the religion." But the treaty had left open the question which edition of the Augsburg Confession should provide this legal basis, and it was no secret to either Roman Catholic or Reformed theologians that important theological differences were reflected in the various editions. In a sense, by placing this decision in the hands of the Protestants the Roman Catholics had cleverly sown the seeds of dissent among the Protestants in such a way as to force them to look ridiculous in terms of the treaty. For if the choice fell to the Unaltered Augsburg Confession of 1530, the exclusion of the Zwinglians and of the Calvinists, who had allied themselves with the Zwinglians through the Consensus Tigurinus *a writing of 1549 by Calvin* of 1549, automatically followed. On the other hand, if the Altered Augsburg Confession of 1540 was acceptable to the Lutherans, they had no choice but to accept as brothers at the Lord's Table those Reformed who were willing to subscribe to this edition with its more ambiguous formulations.

This quandary forced all parties into making not only a theological decision but also one freighted with political consequences. The stricter Lutherans thought themselves conscience-bound to make a theological decision for the Unaltered Augsburg Confession, thus making themselves responsible for the political consequence of excluding Reformed Protestants from the Peace, while at the same time protecting their own political interests. Those Lutherans who hesitated to invite such a cruel consequence for their Reformed brothers felt themselves forced either to compromise their theological convictions or to make the "discovery" that there were no substantive theological differences between themselves and the Reformed. And finally the Reformed were forced either to concede the truth of the Unaltered Augsburg Confession in order thus to enjoy political peace or, which for the conscientious was the more likely, to forego such peace and maintain their own theological integrity at the risk of persecution. Yet insofar as they hesitated to include condemnations in their confessions, they exhibited some of their own politically based considerations.[10] In addition, the fact that nationalistic tendencies were stronger in those lands inclined toward the Reformed faith makes it possible for us to suppose that armed revolution against the emperor for the ostensible reason of preserving "Reformed" theological integrity could also very nicely serve welcome nationalistic ends.—It is a moot question whether the Peace of Augsburg of 1555 should better be qualified with the word "Religious" or the word "Political."[11]

An important nontheological factor contributing toward the emergence of the Center-Party was certainly the political self-consciousness of a leader like Duke Christoph of Wuerttemberg. As we shall see below, his political vision participated perfectly in the ecclesiastical vision of Jakob Andreae and vice versa.

To mention only one more of the secular factors contributing to the formation of the three theological groupings mentioned above, who would doubt the sociological effect which the common border between "Reformed" Switzerland and "Lutheran" Wuerttemberg had on the population of that region? To this day the liturgy of the Lutheran Church in Wuerttemberg betrays a strongly Reformed influence, in sharp contrast, for instance, to the liturgy of the Lutheran Church of Bavaria, which shares a common border with Roman Catholic Austria. What we see in each instance is a Lutheran interpretation given to the prevailing socially induced circumstances in a given locality. Thus it is not at all surprising that the impulse for the building of a Center-Party should have originated in Wuerttemberg with a prince like Christoph and a theologian like Andreae. They understood what it meant to have to face in two directions.

Before proceeding directly with an investigation of the lives of Jakob Andreae, Martin Chemnitz, David Chytraeus, and Nikolaus Selnecker, it would be helpful to have before us a brief sketch of those political/ecclesiastical events subsequent to the Peace of Augsburg which signal the progressive stages leading to the eventual publication of the Formula of Concord.

The Council of Trent, 1545—63. Held during intervals extending from 10 years before the Peace of Augsburg to nearly 10 years after, this council played an important role in the revival of Roman Catholicism, and it helped to mobilize the Counter-Reformation. By its anathematization of doctrinal positions enunciated by the Augsburg Confession it tended to move beyond debate certain positions which the Augsburg Confession itself had not expressly condemned. Thus it contributed toward making vulnerable many of the mildly Romanizing formulations of the Philippists.

The Colloquy at Worms, 1557. The alleged purpose of this colloquy was to give expression to Duke Christoph's policy of presenting a united Lutheran front in the face of the Roman Catholic opposition. He favored a renewed subscription to the Augsburg Confession as interpreted by the Apology and a general condemnation of all opposing doctrines. The Gnesio-Lutherans, however, insisted on specific condemnations. The colloquy ended when the cleft between the Gnesio-Lutherans and the Philippists became so manifest that the Roman Catholic representatives refused to deal with such as could not agree as to who indeed were the true adherents of the Augsburg Confession.

The Frankfurt Recess, 1558. Since the Colloquy at Worms had left the Lutherans in a state of disarray, the Lutheran princes determined to bend all their energies toward healing the breach and restoring religious unity within their churches. They met at Frankfurt/Main in the absence of the theologians and signed the Frankfurt Recess, in which they again solemnly pledged their adherence to the Augsburg Confession of 1530 and its Apology. In an additional four articles they dealt with the controverted questions but in vague and ambiguous terms reflecting the position of Melanchthon. Although readily accepted in Wuerttemberg, there was strong opposition to the Recess in Ernestine Saxony.

The Weimar Book of Confutation, 1559. The Gnesio-Lutheran opposition to the Frankfurt Recess produced the "Weimar Book of Confutation," which made a special point of refuting and rejecting the errors of the Philippists. This in turn spurred on the latter to produce the *Corpus Misnicum* or *Philippicum*, which canonized certain writings of Melanchthon. The breach now seemed incurable and permanent.

The Convention of Princes at Naumburg, 1561. Duke Christoph again urged a convention of princes as the best means to restore unity to Lutheranism. The request of the Gnesio-Lutherans for a free, general Lutheran synod was rejected, and the princes met alone at Naumburg (30 miles southwest of Leipzig) to renew their subscription to the Augsburg Confession. The original intention was to subscribe the unaltered edition, but Elector Frederick III of the Palatinate (who later became a Calvinist) preferred the altered edition of 1540, and his opinion prevailed except with John Frederick of Ernestine Saxony, who refused to sign and left the diet in anger.

The Heidelberg Catechism, 1563. Written by Kaspar Olevianus, pupil of Calvin, and Zacharias Ursinus, pupil of Melanchthon, this catechism was commissioned by Frederick III, elector and ruler of the Palatinate, who by this time had publicly become a supporter of Reformed theology and had embarked upon a determined effort to de-Lutheranize the Palatinate in every particular. Duke Christoph's attempt at the Maulbronn Colloquy (1564) to regain Elector Frederick for his pan-Protestant front against the Romanists ended in failure. The Palatinate was thus lost to Lutheranism except for the brief period of the reign of Ludwig VI (1576—83).

The events marking the stage-by-stage development of the Formula of Concord itself will be dealt with in the chapter treating the foremost author and coordinator of the entire project, Jakob Andreae, so we turn our attention then to the main subject of this study—the formulators of the Formula of Concord.

JAKOB ANDREAE
—THE SUPPLANTER?

There is hardly a Lutheran clergyman who even though he may have long forgotten precisely why it is true nevertheless remembers as indisputable fact that "if Martin Chemnitz had not come along, Martin Luther would hardly have survived." But the person who perhaps sought such praise more than Chemnitz was a man closely associated with him for a period of 12 years (1568—80), Jakob (James) Andreae, without whom it could just as certainly be said there would have been no Formula of Concord. Measured then by the comparative praise bestowed on each of them by subsequent generations, could one say that it was just luck that Chemnitz was baptized Martin whereas Andreae was christened Jakob (meaning "he supplants"—Gen. 25:26)?

Or if the reason for the distinction in the reputations of the two men lies deeper than the fact that Chemnitz shares a name (and but for one day a birthday) with Luther, is it perhaps in keeping with "changing times, changing customs" that our own generation with its self-conscious realism about the role of political tactics in the ongoing business of the institutional church might be expected to generate more interest in Andreae than in Chemnitz? Will Andreae be more highly appreciated at the tetracentenary of the Formula of Concord than at the time of its initial publication?

There are questions enough, then, to arouse our interest in this man who has been shaping the life of Lutheranism ever since "the Formula of Concord was signed by the electors of Saxony, of Brandenburg, and of the Palatinate; furthermore by 20 dukes and princes, 24 counts, 4 barons, 35 imperial cities, and about 8,000 pastors and teachers"[1] by the date of its publication, spectacularly timed (or providentially planned) for June 25, 1580, the 50th anniversary of the presentation of the Augsburg Confession to Charles V.

Born in Waiblingen (five miles east-northeast of Stuttgart) on the

Festival of the Annunciation of the Blessed Virgin Mary (March 25) in the year 1528, Jakob Andreae lived out his life as one controlled by the events shaping that date and that year in the history of the Reformation. Waiblingen being located in the duchy of Wuerttemberg, it is not too likely that Andreae's father, a blacksmith, went to Mass that day to gain divine favor through the Blessed Virgin for his newly born son. For Wuerttemberg had been exposed to a great deal of Evangelical preaching by this time through the influence of men like Brenz, Schnepf, Alber, and Blarer, and anti-Catholic feeling ran very high. But had Andreae's father taught young Jakob to attend Mass on his birthday, the latter would have heard the words of Mary heralding the beginning of each new year of his life: "Behold, I am the handmaid of the Lord; let it be to me according to Your word."

That Andreae felt himself especially singled out by Providence is clear from the numerous references he makes to how God saved him on various occasions from drowning and from other injuries or death as the result of accidents. But few of his contemporaries felt that he lived as the "servant of the Lord" as much as he lived in the service of the princely courts and of his own ambition.[2] Perhaps the two are inseparable in his case.

Several history-shaping events in the year 1528 seem also to stand as beacons directing the course of Andreae's development. It was the year of Luther's "Large Confession" regarding the Sacrament of the Altar, part of which found its way into the Schwabach Articles of 1529 and thence into the Augsburg Confession. It is considered by some scholars the greatest work on this subject ever written, and it served as the theological base from which Luther confronted Zwingli the following year at Marburg.[3] More than any other doctrine it was, as we shall see, the doctrine concerning the Lord's Supper and its Christological corollary which held the key to Andreae's theological development and his concordistic activity. And the conviction that the faith must be confessed stuck with him to the end.

The year 1528 was also of particular importance in Waiblingen itself. Berthold Aichelin had been appointed inquisitor by his Roman Catholic superiors in the Swabian League, and he held court over Anabaptists supposedly harbored there as well as in the surrounding towns.[4] Andreae himself would later become involved in a less bloody but hardly more tolerant anti-Anabaptist action as he labored toward introducing an implementable church discipline in his congregation and

20

elsewhere. One thing Andreae never seemed to be, and that was soft on "enthusiasts."

Finally, the year of Andreae's birth was also the year revealing the results of the first great church visitation in Saxony. To meet the need Melanchthon had prepared the "Instruction of the Visitors to the Pastors" and Luther had supplied the preface. Among other things this ordinance summarized the Evangelical doctrines in a simplified form and provided for their enforcement by threat of banishment. Melanchthon's chief concern was to educate the clergy into a dependable and unified organ in the service of a Christian government.[5] It was with this page from Melanchthon's book in his hand (or at least in his unconscious) that Andreae 40 years later met his new co-worker, Chemnitz, in Brunswick to conduct the visitation for Duke Julius there. This association with Chemnitz then ushered in the climactic phase of Andreae's concordistic activity.

So in more than one way March 25, 1528, marked the birth of the child that was the father of the man Jakob Andreae.

The Child

When Johann Valentin Andreae (1586—1654) published a biography of his, for some famous but for many infamous, grandfather Jakob,[6] he was patently enjoying the recognition accorded a family of the nobility. For Jakob himself it was different, and he frequently had to defend himself against the *argumentum ad hominem* which would not let him forget his humble origin as the son of a former mercenary soldier and blacksmith. The "Bidembach brothers" at the ducal court in Stuttgart enjoyed exploiting the natural inferiority feelings of this parvenu, who at an early age seemed to have captured the attention of princes and lords, by referring to him as "Smithy" or "Jack the Smith."[7]

His formal education began at the age of six, but financial difficulties soon threatened to force him to exchange his academic career for a carpenter's workshop. Was it then providence, luck, or "politics" which enabled him to receive a "ducal" scholarship? At any rate, shortly after his 11th birthday he continued his basic education at the Paedagogium in Stuttgart in preparation for matriculation two years later (1541) at the University in Tuebingen. Already at Stuttgart and then again at Tuebingen he enjoyed the attention given him by Erhard Schnepf (1495—1558), a Lutheran theologian and church administrator highly

1495-1558

21

respected at the court of Duke Ulrich of Wuerttemberg. The latter once said of Andreae: "No matter where this young man may stem from, there is no doubt but that Schnepf hatched him."[8]

By 1543 Andreae had earned his bachelor's degree and two years later, when only 17 years old and as the second-ranking student in the class, his master's. Among his fellow students was David Chytraeus, who earned his master's degree the preceding year at the extremely tender age of 14.[9]

It would seem that in those days "childhood" in the sense of economic and educational dependency was not permitted to linger on until a person's 20s. In the year 1546, about three months after Luther's death,[10] Andreae was requested by his ecclesiastical superiors to break off his theological studies of just one year's duration in order to accept his first pastoral office in Stuttgart. He was then 18 years old and inclined to marry. He did—a Johanna Entringer, the 20-year-old daughter of a distinguished Tuebingen burgher, praised for her thrift and piety. She bore him 18 children, nine sons and nine daughters, before she preceded him in death by seven years in 1583.

The Father

As pastor in Stuttgart and as head of an ever-growing family, Andreae soon had an opportunity to test his calling as "servant of the Lord." Within a year the defeat of Wuerttemberg in the Smalcald War (1547) brought to Stuttgart the Spanish army of occupation; and of all the evangelical clergymen there, he was the only one not to abandon his post, until a year later when the introduction of the Interim (1548) forced Duke Ulrich to send him to Tuebingen.

By this time he was already the father of two children and experiencing an overtaxed budget. Again the good will of the ducal court met his need and thus bound this grateful man even more intimately to itself. But as a result Andreae was able to matriculate at the University once more and continue his doctoral studies.

Meanwhile he also resumed his preaching activity, and it soon became clear that he really excelled at this task. To protect him from the implementers of the Interim, members of his congregation, composed largely of university students, accompanied him as a bodyguard to and from the church. Once the abbot at the cloister in nearby Bebenhausen threatened to have his salary withheld if he continued his polemics against the Mass, but Andreae did not submit to this intimidation. Nor did he meekly permit the charge that he had publicly compared the emperor to Nero to go unanswered. His conduct at this time seems to leave no doubt that though he was willing to be a "servant of the duke," he was this only insofar as he could thereby be a "servant of the Lord."

About this time Andreae made the personal acquaintance of Johannes Brenz at the home of his godfather Leonhard Fuchs, and it was Brenz who, as chief administrator of the "duke's church," soon was able to involve his newly found "disciple" in official theological tasks as assigned by the court. Duke Christoph, who had succeeded his father Ulrich in office in 1550, now insisted that Andreae obtain his doctorate with financial assistance from the ducal treasury, and in appreciation thereof Andreae declared himself willing to assume a new assignment as pastor in Goeppingen, about 30 miles east-southeast of Stuttgart. There he was active for 10 years (1552—62), advancing to the position of general superintendent and meanwhile also acquiring his degree of doctor of sacred theology in 1553.[11]

The Goeppingen years were for Andreae a period of testing. Whose man was he? God's, the duke's, the emperor's? Was he his own man capable also of growing beyond himself or was he caught and locked within himself and within his times? A number of incidents will serve to illustrate the result of this testing process.

Ever since the treaty of Kaaden in 1534, when Duke Ulrich had his land returned to him as a fief from Catholic Austria, he was bound to hold to the Augsburg Confession and not to tolerate "Sacramentarians" in his land. Kaspar Schwenkfeld qualified for such "nontoleration," and so it is not altogether surprising that soon after taking up his duties at Goeppingen Andreae initiated a correspondence with Schwenkfeld in which he called into question the latter's doctrine of the invisibility of the church, citing against him Matt. 18:17 ("tell it to the church") and concluding from this verse that the church of Jesus Christ must be visible. But Schwenkfeld stood his ground, not even retreating before the proof passage hurled at him, and he countered by asking Andreae where this church was in which the impenitent brother was considered a "Gentile and a tax collector." Andreae didn't seem to miss the point, because within a short time he and his brother-in-law, Caspar Leyser, were putting their heads together as to how they might introduce a more effective form of church discipline within their congregations.[12]

Before long, letters were being exchanged with Calvin on the one hand and Duke Christoph on the other, and it is not insignificant that the upshot of the whole affair was a synod in 1554 at which in effect, at the instance of Brenz, the riot act was read to Andreae and Leyser. They were required to conform to the ecclesiastical law and order of the official church regulation of 1553 or else. Here excommunication was a matter to be regulated not by the individual pastor and/or his parish, but it was the exclusive responsibility of the duke's synodical consistory.[13] Brenz was putting Andreae to the test. Would he also be the duke's servant or not? Andreae said, "I will." For Andreae, of course, this did not necessarily mean that he would not be God's servant but merely that in order to be the latter he would agree to be the former.

There is another incident occurring about this time which some Lutherans would rather forget, since it illustrates so dramatically the extent to which Andreae was a product and prisoner of his own culture even though he could revel in the freedom of the Gospel. To this extent, like Luther and the apostle Paul before him, he was an evangelical prophet speaking God's word from within and to his own culture and not an apocalyptic figure speaking from beyone history.[14] The story, in brief, is this:[15]

> A Jew by the name of Ansteet was sentenced to die by hanging from his feet. His crime—robbery. Roman Catholic priests were present at the hanging, attempting to convert the Jew to the Christian faith. He stubbornly refused, so two dogs were hung by their feet, one on either side of him. They began to assuage their pain by snapping at the Jew, biting off his ears and gnawing at his elbows. He begged for mercy but the priests admonished him to believe in Jesus. He refused. Finally Andreae was summoned from the crowd of onlookers to try his skill at converting the condemned man. At first Andreae refused since he felt the priests had sufficiently and correctly enough preached Christ to the Jew. But at the insistence of his friends he relented. He preached Jesus Christ to him but did so restricting himself entirely to the Old Testament. This method met with success and the Jew asked to receive Christian baptism. He was baptized while hanging in the upside-down position, confessing Jesus as Messiah. Then he was hung properly by the neck and so died saved, as all hoped, by his faith in the Lord Jesus.

This story is not related in order to depict Andreae as an anti-Semite in a racist sense. He was this demonstrably only in a religious sense. But the incident does reflect the degree to which Andreae was still a captive of his culture, which had not yet developed more humane methods of dealing with dissenters. On the one hand Andreae could quote St. Augustine against Roman Catholics and their practice of forced conversion, but then again he could cite the same Augustine as witness against the pacifist appeals of the Anabaptists, arguing that though one cannot force faith one nevertheless ought not despise any means whereby God might give the gift of faith. The apostle Paul served as authoritative Biblical illustration—first God "forced" him to the ground with a blinding light and then he "taught" him the Gospel.

Why relate this incident?—The lessons of history ought to be recalled even when they prove embarrassing. A wholesome effect would occur if we could recognize our continuity with the imperfection and sins of our fathers, repent, and hear the Gospel. Secondly, we could be forcefully reminded that neither Christ, nor His Gospel, nor His church is a nonworldly phantom bearing only the appearance of the world. The formulators of the Formula of Concord share in this rootedness in history. They were in the world and to some extent also of the world, but they confessed that they were saved by that grace of God which came into the world and participated in the world. Understood thus, the story conveys much more than a preview of the mentality with which Andreae appeared to implement the acceptance of the Formula of Concord some 25 years later. [16]

A political event of watershed significance occurred during Andreae's ministry in Goeppingen. The Peace of Augsburg (1555) went into effect with its principle that "He who owns the land determines the religion." Only adherents of the Augsburg Confession were to enjoy the privileges that the new law provided. "Sacramentarians," i. e., Zwinglians and Calvinists, and "sectarians," i. e., Anabaptists, were not included in the peace. Imagine what that meant! When Andreae began his ministry in Goeppingen (1552), the exchange of letters which Leyser and he had with Calvin had no obvious political significance. [17] After 1555, however, friendly epistolary exchanges between Lutherans and Calvinists became charged with political dynamite. Lutherans became more intolerant of Calvinistic views lest they risk losing their political advantage, and Calvinists became more suspicious of Lutheran offers to "dialog," suspecting that the Lutherans would make no concessions which might jeopardize their own political advantage. All of Andreae's subsequent ecclesiastical activity must be viewed with the implications of the Peace of Augsburg in mind. [18]

In 1556 Andreae was authorized by Duke Christoph to assist with the introduction of the Lutheran Reformation in the Pforzheim portion of the Margravate of Baden (about 35 miles northwest of Stuttgart). This activity has particular significance because it serves as a preview of Andreae's later conflicts with the theologians from Saxony. Representatives of the latter, who were also assisting with the Reformation in Baden, charged Brenz with teaching incorrectly concerning justification, Baptism, the Lord's Supper, and the descent into hell. On all counts Andreae defended Brenz and to some extent also Osiander, whose novel theology had received a favorable interpretation from Brenz. Most of the differences are simply written off by Andreae as misunderstandings of infelicitous expressions. In other words, Andreae believed he could establish agreement by working at the problems as though they were basically "semantic" in nature. For instance, by clear thinking and the making of distinctions he could harmonize opposing assertions such as:

> Christ justifies us according to His divine nature alone.
> Christ justifies us according to His human nature alone.

These two statements, he would argue, are not contradictory when one distinguishes between different kinds of causes. The former is the "efficient cause," the latter is the "instrumental cause."[19]

Although not all theologians would be satisfied with Andreae's solution and although not all problems would allow solution by such a method, one must admit that Andreae contributed to a truly ecumenical spirit when he urged clear, unimpassioned thinking as one means of eliminating specious problems dividing Christian brothers. Yet he did not put excessive faith in this method since he also distinguished between "school theology" and "church theology" and warned against introducing problems arising in the former into the sphere of the latter, which for him was composed for the "simple layman."[20] Andreae, no less than we, knew the gulf which often divides the theologian's theology from the simple Christian's faith. Was his advice not to "confuse" the layman a cop-out before the theological task, or was it good care of souls by an experienced pastor? Or was it neither but rather church-political realism?—Certainly we ought not encourage the heretical notion of a double truth, but the apostle Paul does distinguish between milk and solid food.[21]

Andreae's ministry in Goeppingen coincided with those years of Duke Christoph's rule (1550—68) during which he was developing and supporting an interconfessional and federative policy of strengthening the empire by stabilizing the peace between the confessions. To achieve this end, he desired a church united in its adherence to the Augsburg Confession, but this presupposed a "normative exposition" of this Confession. To forestall theological controversies, he favored book censorship and strict governmental surveillance of theologians' activities. The theological distillations of Andreae deriving from this period are expressive of his accommodating himself, apparently without inner struggle, to these church-political ambitions of Christoph. He did this not by compromising the content of his theology as such but by placing the accents in such a way that Christoph's interests would be furthered. [22]

A good illustration of this is Andreae's very first publication. The fact that it deals with the controversy concerning the Lord's Supper is symptomatic, for it was that subject which more than any other would come to dominate Andreae's theological thinking and ultimately also the theology of the Formula of Concord. Appearing in the year 1557, it shared new publication notices with Calvin's *Second Defense . . . Against . . . Joachim Westphal.* [23] This was also the year of the Worms Colloquy, at which the deep disunity existing in the Protestant camp was disclosed as the Roman Catholic theologians skillfully exposed the discrepancies between the Augsburg Confession of 1530 and the Altered Augsburg Confession of 1540. Their strategy was to entice the Protestants into condemning each other, and into this trap the Gnesio-Lutherans ran with confessional zeal.

It was at this point that Andreae seemed to recognize the need for an all-out effort to restore unity among Lutherans. He saw that he would have to alter his own strategy as reflected in his first Lord's Supper publication, where his differences with Calvin were so subtly phrased that he could hope that Lutherans and Calvinists alike would approve of the writing. But he was to be disappointed on both scores. [24] Though he of all Lutherans of his time came closest to maintaining a friendly, open spirit of dialog with his Calvinist counterparts, he now began to realize more and more at least the political necessity of accenting not only agreements but at first gently and then ever more firmly also differences. His theological commitments often seemed to come only after political realities and personal ambitions had made clear the course he wished to follow.

Calvin's last letter to Andreae (1558) gives evidence of how he and the Swiss theologians read the behavior of the Lutherans subsequent to the Peace of Augsburg. They felt that the Lutherans were hiding behind the Augsburg Confession as an umbrella which they used to shield their pampered and sleepy selves from the heat of persecution. They too desired peace but not such as was obtained at the cost of sound doctrine or by injuring members of the body of Christ (meant are the Zwinglians who had been condemned by the Lutherans, including Melanchthon, at the Worms Colloquy). At any rate Calvin hoped that Andreae would at Frankfurt (1558) support Beza's request for political assistance for the persecuted French brethren. [25]

This last thought, which hints at the beginning of the wars of religion in western Europe, must now be assessed at greater length since it contributed greatly to Andreae's ultimate self-understanding. The question has to do with Andreae's relationship to the Calvinists. If before 1559 Andreae was not altogether convinced that Calvin's doctrine of the Sacrament was theologically untenable, events in 1559 helped him come to a more committed decision. Winds of political revolution were beginning to blow harder in France, England, Spain, and Italy. The death of Henry II in France signaled the increase of rivalry between the Huguenots and the House of Guise. And with the Calvinization of the Palatinate, the territory of Wuerttemberg was being surrounded by a wing of the Reformation which was leaning more and more toward accepting the propriety of armed resistance to secure certain religio-political rights. For this development Duke Christoph had no stomach. [26]

But did Andreae? In no way. Yet to prove it he was put to the test also in regard to his doctrine of the Lord's Supper, lest perhaps this be the door through which the Reformed would entice him into their circle, and once there Andreae would, so one might suspect, also share the spirit of the political revolutionaries in their midst. [27] The test took place in the context of a synod at which Andreae was to conduct the hearing of a certain Hagen of Dettingen, being tried for Calvinizing tendencies. It was hoped that his conducting of the case would betray his own position. Although he dealt sympathetically and kindly with Hagen, the upshot of this so-called "Stuttgart Synod" (1559) was the formulation of a confession which made the doctrine of the ubiquity of Christ's human nature binding upon all pastors in Wuerttemberg. [28] Andreae not only passed the test but in the process he became instrumental in making the ubiquity doctrine a test question for orthodoxy in Lutheranism. [29] And at the same time his future course thereby came into view: Though at one with Melanchthon's school in the struggle for doctrinal peace and unity, the theological gulf between the two continued to widen; on the other hand, though generally in theological agreement with the Gnesio-Lutherans, his "conciliation politics" developed as a bone of contention between them.[30]

During his last year as general superintendent at Goeppingen, Andreae was sent by Christoph to participate in the Colloquy of Poissy (1561). Arriving late, he was only able to engage in some of the unimportant closing sessions. It did not take him long to realize that the French climate was not suited to German-cultured "ubiquity" seedlings and that the political winds were far too gusty for him to sail his "made in Lutheran Germany" ecclesiastical bark there. He was too much of a mind with the political goals of the loyal imperialist Christoph to find congenial the brand of hypernationalistic Protestantism growing on French soil. The superintendent from Goeppingen chose to sacrifice dreams of an international Protestantism in order not to lose an elusive but still not impossible united German Lutheran church flourishing as *religio licita* within the Holy Roman Empire of the German Nation.

The year 1561 brought to Andreae an expression of the confidence which his conduct up to that point had won for him in the eyes of Duke Christoph. The latter appointed him chancellor of the University of Tuebingen as well as assigning him to the accompanying posts of professor of theology and diocesan provost, positions he held the rest of his life. The man whose father had once been numbered among the emperor's "smiths," himself now served as one of the duke's *Spitzenreiter* ("top riders"). The heady air in which he presently found himself could not but have an effect on the man who within 34 years moved from an atmosphere of cultural rags to one of cultural riches.

Among Andreae's colleagues were Dietrich Schnepf, son of the idol of his youth; Jakob Heerbrand, who had studied in Wittenberg under Luther and Melanchthon and who himself wrote a popular *Compendium theologiae;* and the younger Johannes Brenz, son of Duke Christoph's trusted adviser—a formidable theological faculty from which Christoph could expect and did receive a university dominated by orthodox Lutheranism.[31]

When present in Tuebingen, which frequently was only for short periods of time, Andreae lectured on the letters of the New Testament and Melanchthon's *Loci* or Heerbrand's *Compendium*. He excelled at conducting disputations, but particularly at preaching. At least three times a month he would preach at the Tuebingen collegiate church. As chancellor he was committed to representing the concerns of the duke before both students and faculty and to implementing these concerns. Once he had to arbitrate a town-gown conflict when some weapon-wielding students on a high made their presence unappreciated by the Tuebingen citizenry. All in all he was one of Lutheranism's most active and productive personages ever.[32]

So involved was Andreae as the duke's ecclesiastical representative and troubleshooter that before he could even assume his new duties in Tuebingen he was sent off to Weimar to help adjudicate the case of Victorin Strigel, professor at Jena, whom the Gnesio-Lutherans accused of heresy in reference to the doctrine of the bondage of the will, but whom Duke John Frederick II wished to rehabilitate as a sign that ecclesiastical jurisdiction lay with him and his appointed consistory rather than with a theological faculty or, as the followers of Flacius wanted it, with the local parish pastor(s). Andreae, of course, had been through the question of church discipline before,[33] and he had learned his lesson so well that Christoph now was pleased to send him to Weimar as a favor to Duke John Frederick II. Christoph was confident that Andreae would see to it that the Gnesio-Lutherans back off and that John Frederick be enabled to inaugurate a religious politics more to Christoph's own liking.

As it turned out, Strigel played the game of theological semantics well and thus was able temporarily, at least, to secure his reputation as an orthodox theologian by playing into the hands of John Frederick II and Christoph with their ecclesiastical politics. Though the astuteness of an Andreae should not have permitted him to be deceived by Strigel's "playing" (a less pejorative and perhaps more sensitive description might be "wrestling") with the meaning of active and passive when applied to man's "capacity" or "aptitude" for conversion,[34] he too apparently played the game along with the others, following suit after his duke, who had led off. In general one can detect in Andreae a more consistent application of his discriminatory ability in the realm of Christology rather than in that of anthropology. The doctrine of the Lord's Supper fascinated him more than that of justification. But again this may have been the result more of his commitment to Christoph's politics than an expression of theological one-sidedness.[35]

One of the fateful consequences of Andreae's involvement in the Strigel case was that he thereby lost the confidence of the Gnesio-Lutherans, who then became a core of resistance to his concordistic activity six years later. Already in 1563, when a certain Alexius

Bresnitzer accused him of causing offense by his conduct in the Strigel case, Andreae excused himself by saying he was merely carrying out "ducal orders," to which Bresnitzer replied that he should feel himself more bound to Christ than to the duke.[36] A fitting reminder to this "servant of the Lord"!

After his return from Weimar, Andreae had just enough time to settle in Tuebingen and get the feel of his new position as University Chancellor, etc., when a new ducal order (1563) sent him to Strassburg, where he was to mediate in a controversy between two of the local professors, the Lutheran Johann Marbach and the more Calvinistically inclined Hieronymus Zanchi. The latter had been maneuvered by Marbach into subscribing to the Augsburg Confession, but he did so only with the qualification "as correctly understood," which for him meant insofar as it agreed with the Tetrapolitana, the confession prepared by Bucer and Capito and presented separately to the emperor at Augsburg in 1530 as the rule of faith of the four South German imperial cities, one of which was Strassburg. Now Zanchi was being accused by Marbach of teaching incorrectly concerning the Lord's Supper and predestination, the latter being a new subject of controversy among the Protestants. In the hope that the dispute could be settled and that Zanchi could be proven loyal to the Augsburg Confession and thus supportive of Christoph's religious politics, Andreae was sent by the duke to the scene to do his thing—clarify and, if possible, remove differences.

Perhaps Andreae sensed that some differences are "removed" more quickly by avoiding clarification of positions. At any rate, as soon as Zanchi agreed that Christ is present in the Sacrament in such a way as to communicate Himself to the recipient in a spiritual fashion, Andreae was quick to build on this "concession" and not to push Zanchi on acceptance of the *manducatio oralis* (reception of the presence of Christ by oral eating), which Andreae unexpectedly conceded is not meant to mean that "the body of Christ touches our mouth and body . . . but that he and others speak in some such fashion only because of the sacramental union."[37] Zanchi acknowledged the *manducatio impiorum* (reception of the presence of Christ by the unworthy) only insofar as this implied the weak in faith, not however those who were manifestly unworthy. This also Andreae was willing to tolerate since there was agreement on "the true and substantial presence" of Christ and he was confident that with time Zanchi also would come to "our viewpoint." Meanwhile he did not consider the difference between their positions as being "great."[38] Thus at this juncture Andreae did not insist upon an interpretation of the "sacramental union" in terms of its consequences, namely, the "oral eating" and the "eating by the unworthy." This understanding was later to be required by the Formula of Concord.[39] However, for the present these were dispensable theological opinions not particularly suited to serving the religio-political interests of Christoph and his faithful theologian Andreae.

Similarly, in the discussion between Zanchi and Andreae on the question of predestination, an understanding was reached only on the minimum requirements for agreement, and even these remained ambiguous. Whereas Lutherans were suspicious of the "theology of benefits" which characterized the Reformed view of the sacraments, the Reformed, in turn, were chary of the same approach in the Lutheran view of predestination. Lutherans felt that the Reformed by their spiritualizing tendencies were in danger of losing the ontological basis for the benefits of Christ in the Sacrament, whereas the Reformed missed precisely such an ontological basis for the benefits which Lutherans ascribed to predestination. They felt that Lutherans spiritualized predestination by making it a function of the means of grace rather than emphasizing its basis in the absolute and eternal will of God. But Andreae and Zanchi left these problems unresolved. Apparently to their thinking the ambiguities did not necessarily imperil the Gospel, whereas to have removed the ambiguities would have imperiled chances of achieving Protestant unity and its political corollary. Yet Zanchi felt strongly enough about his own position that he signed the "Strassburg Formula" only conditionally, stating: "I accept this doctrinal formula insofar as I understand it to be correct."[40] It is of interest to note that experiences with such conditional subscriptions as the above probably prompted Andreae in 1577, when writing Elector August of Saxony as to procedures for gaining approval of the "Bergic Book" (Formula of Concord), to advise the obtaining of signatures with no additions other than place of residence and title.[41] For soon after giving his qualified signature to the Strassburg Formula Zanchi was assuring Calvin that his subscription absolved him from accepting anything in the Formula with which he did not agree.

Both Andreae and Christoph were pleased with their "success" at Strassburg, so much so that they felt the time was ripe to approach King Maximilian with a written formulation of their unification plans (1563). Though at this time no answer was forthcoming from Maximilian, who was known to have Protestant sympathies, seven years later when Duke Julius of Brunswick had Andreae accompany him to Prague, Andreae was invited to an audience with Maximilian II, who by this time had become emperor (1564—96). There was hardly anything which could have bolstered his self-confidence more than this honor, and he continued to use it to good advantage. [42]

For instance, in 1564 Andreae was commissioned by Christoph to head the delegation of Wuerttemberg theologians sent to Maulbronn to discuss with theologians from the Palatinate, in the presence of Duke Christoph and Elector Frederick III, the pros and cons of the Heidelberg Catechism, which had just appeared during the previous year. He defended the doctrine of the majesty of the man Jesus and the use of the term "ubiquity," arguing that the term originated with the opponents of the doctrine and though it did not appear in Scripture, which, as he pointed out, was also true of the word *homoousios,* nevertheless what the word signified was clearly taught by Scripture. He proposed that Jesus' human nature is not destroyed by ubiquity, as the Heidelberg theologians charged, but that it is rather enhanced by it. He, in turn, charged the Heidelberg delegation with reducing Christ to a mere man. Though the Maulbronn discussions did not lead to a consensus, they triggered a burst of literary activity between Tuebingen and Heidelberg in the process of which Andreae is said to have developed a deeper appreciation for the purely human, historical figure of Christ. This could, if it were true, be characterized as an advance beyond the Christology of Brenz. Yet Andreae was interpreted by his contemporary opponents as a genuine representative of Brenz's position. [43]

The years between 1564 and 1568 found Andreae working closer to home than what for him as ducal representative had become normal. It was a period of fruitful literary activity, with his publications striking in all directions—a comprehensive Christology, polemical tracts against papists, sermons, popular symbolics, and comparative religion. Of particular interest is the last category, as represented by his apology of the Christian faith over against Mohammedanism. After studying the original text of the Koran, Andreae felt qualified to state that the Christology represented there, namely, Christ as a man who loved, was like that of his opponents among the Philippists and Calvinists.

That was the Christological, anti-enthusiast, confessional challenge of this "servant of the Lord" whose life as child and father we have considered. Indeed, the child was father of this man.

The Man

The year 1568 marked the beginning of the mature and climactic phase of the now 40-year-old Jakob Andreae. Already since the Worms Colloquy of 1557 he had been convinced of the critical need for establishing unity among the quarreling Lutherans lest they forfeit the privileges accorded them by the Peace of Augsburg. [44] By 1561 Duke Christoph had prepared a document for the upcoming Naumburg Assembly of princes in which he outlined the plan later to be executed as the means of effecting a theological concord which would guarantee the peace and further his own political ambitions. [45] Now, just months before his death, he granted Andreae permission to accept the invitation of Duke Julius of Brunswick to join Martin Chemnitz in supervising the reformation of his domains. At the same time he authorized him to use the opportunity to try to effect a union between the Saxon theologians and "other pure churches." [46] This then was to become Andreae's most formidable task, the one to which he devoted the rest of his life, bringing it to a climax with the publication of the Formula of Concord in 1580 and then implementing and defending it for another 10 years until his death in 1590.

These last 22 years of his life, the mature Andreae as concordist, can themselves be subdivided into three stages, each descriptive of a characteristic change in his concordistic activity: (1) Concordia through exchange (1568—70); (2) Concordia through exclusion (1570—77); (3) Concordia through expulsion (1577—90).

1) Concordia Through Exchange (1568—70)

The notion of "exchange" was already in Andreae's briefcase when he arrived in Brunswick in 1568. After a number of preliminary meetings with Duke Julius concerning the church visitation, he nudged the conversation over to the subject which by now had become his passion— the question of how to restore doctrinal unity to Lutheranism. For the eventuality of this meeting with Julius, he had prepared two proposals, each quite different in character. One was written in Latin, and in addition to its positive articulations of the doctrines in question it presented also precise condemnations of the conflicting positions and their authors. The other, far shorter, proposal was written in German and was restricted to making affirmative statements with only broad and general condemnations of "all those who teach otherwise."[47] Thus Andreae indicated both his willingness to exchange one approach for the other as well as his desire to exchange conversation in both directions—with the Gnesio-Lutherans who believed Lutheranism could not live by affirmations alone and with the Philippists who believed that it could.

The proposals were composed of five articles dealing with: (1) justification by faith; (2) good works; (3) free will; (4) adiaphora; (5) the Lord's Supper.[48] Of special interest is the appendix which Andreae had attached to his treatment of the final article. It concerned itself with the question of the ubiquity of Christ and argued that this doctrine was to be adduced only if it became clear that the simple meaning of the words of institution was being rejected because of some theory about Jesus being immobilized at the right hand of God. Thus the astute and now highly experienced ecclesiastical negotiator was able to state a doctrine dear to his religio-political heart and yet indicate his willingness to exchange its mention for a clear-cut statement of the real presence of Christ in the Sacrament.

As promising of success as all this must have appeared to Andreae, he soon was to be unburdened of any illusions. His acquaintance from their days together as students at Tuebingen, David Chytraeus, did not criticize the content or format of the "Five Articles" so much as rather the entire presupposition underlying them, namely, that a new confession in the sense of a *formula concordiae* was desirable.[49] And the Wittenberg theologians indicated that little unity could be achieved so long as there was no agreement on a more comprehensive and binding *corpus doctrinae,* which for them meant a collection of Melanchthon's writings which were raised to near symbolical status by their publication as *Corpus doctrinae Misnicum* in 1560.

Meanwhile Duke Christoph, Andreae's patron and political lord, had died. Andreae, back in Wuerttemberg, had the gratification of obtaining support for his "Five Articles" from his Swabian colleagues; otherwise his success was minimal. But he continued to cultivate the good will of influential princes, and before long (1569) he was once again in Brunswick, this time with the support of Christoph's successor, Duke Ludwig (1567—93), Landgrave William of Hesse (1567—92), and, of course, Duke Julius of Brunswick (1568—89). These united to convince Elector August of Saxony (1553—86) of the importance of inviting Andreae to continue his discussions with the Saxon theologians with a view to achieving agreement. Though Andreae appeared with the backing of four Protestant courts, the Wittenberg theologians remained unimpressed and merely maneuvered Andreae into acknowledging his agreement with their *corpus doctrinae* without their placing themselves squarely behind his articles.

Thus Andreae began to lose more than he was gaining, for opponents of the Philippists felt he had conceded them too much. In Jena his articles were publicly rejected by Duke John William, and in his home town of Tuebingen his colleagues began to think of him as a self-adulating meddler. In Brunswick there was also a noticeable coolness developing in the relationship to Chemnitz, who more and more felt the necessity of insisting upon thesis and antithesis in a confessional statement. Duke Julius attempted to keep doors open on all sides, going so far as to arrange an audience for Andreae with Maximilian II in Prague. [50] But Andreae began to get the same message from all quarters—concordia through exchange will never work. This was so not because the idea itself was ridiculous but because most of his contemporaries were not willing or ready to participate in such exchange. The age of genuine dialog had not yet culturally arrived. [51]

Yet Andreae was willing to make one more attempt at following this approach. The very next year (1570) at Zerbst, 30 miles west of Wittenberg on the road to Brunswick, an assembly of theologians was held at the instance of Duke Julius and Andreae. Here Andreae attempted to make a virtue out of necessity by dropping talk about his "Five Articles" and instead grabbing the criticism which had been made earlier by the Wittenberg theologians as a new point of departure, namely, the need for establishing a recognized *corpus doctrinae*. [52] As confessions generally accepted by all Lutherans there were the Augsburg Confession, its Apology, Luther's Catechisms, and his Smalcald Articles. These even the Wittenberg theologians were willing to recognize as normative, but with a qualification which Andreae unfortunately preferred not to recall, namely, that in contradistinction to his own wish that all other confessions might be normative only insofar as they did not contradict this *corpus doctrinae,* they subscribed to his proposed *corpus doctrinae* only insofar as their own *Corpus Misnicum* would thereby not be considered in any way to have been contradicted or put in second place. [53]

But in all this Andreae seemed primarily to be playing a face-saving game. It was difficult for him to admit without qualification that his "concordia through exchange" approach had failed miserably. Yet in his own mind he knew it had, and already he was settling on a new approach.

2) Concordia Through Exclusion (1570—77)

One of the most hotly disputed issues of Andreae's concordistic activity up to this point was the question as to whether or not or in what form condemnations of opposing doctrines and their authors should appear in new doctrinal confessions. [54] If until the meeting of theologians at Zerbst in 1570 Andreae was more inclined to agree with Duke Christoph, who consistently refused to approve of applying personal condemnations to differing theologians within Germany as long as they did not contradict the notion of a territorial church (as did, for instance, the Anabaptists and Schwenckfeldians), [55] after Zerbst his mind had changed. He saw that trying to exchange opinions with the Philippists was for him a losing game. [56] He had learned that the road to Lutheran unity involved climbing a steeper grade than he had anticipated and that if he was to take this mountain at all he would have to travel more lightly. But what could he leave behind? He decided he would get there fastest and with the most if he gave up trying to include the Philippists, so his new policy of "concordia through exclusion" was inaugurated by dropping the Philippists. Condemnations would now be in, which meant that Philippists would now be out.

This decision was for Andreae a piece of good timing. What could have been more desirable than that Elector August of Saxony should at about this time have begun to reach clarity about the heterodoxy of his own theologians and in a housecleaning mood should have approved precisely of the condemnations which Andreae now had in mind? [57] But this development was as yet an uncertainty for Andreae, and so depressed was he about the prospect of success for his concordistic activity that he turned his attention briefly to the East and took an energetic part in the correspondence of the Lutheran theologians of Tuebingen with the Ecumenical Patriarch, Jeremiah II (1536—95).

In 1573 Andreae made the first move to carry out his new policy of exclusion by publishing (it cannot be determined whether they were ever preached) sermons on the doctrines controverted among the adherents to the Augsburg Confession. These *Six Christian Sermons* dealt with justification, good works, original sin, free will, adiaphora, Law and Gospel, and the Person of Christ in relation to the doctrine of the Lord's Supper. They did not hesitate to include the condemnation of false doctrines, even going so far as to cite the names of their proponents, e. g., Osiander, Major, Flacius, Strigel, Agricola, and the "new

Wittenbergians."[58] Andreae dedicated the sermons to his chief supporter among the princes at the moment, Duke Julius of Brunswick, and he sent copies to Chemnitz and Chytraeus in the hope of obtaining through them the approval of the Lower Saxons. The clergy of Wuerttemberg and his colleagues at Tuebingen once again became supportive by lending signatures and a letter commending his effort to unite the churches of Swabia and Saxony.[59]

At last Andreae seemed to be speaking a language close to the hearts of the North German theologians. Chemnitz and Chytraeus had nothing explicit to criticize as to the doctrinal content of the *Sermons,* yet they thought that the sermonic form ought to be replaced by more precisely stated theses and antitheses.[60] Andreae hastened to comply, almost giving the impression that he feared someone else might beat him to it and he would at best then have to share the honors as author. For these articles, known as the "Swabian Concordia" (1574), he again hurriedly obtained signatures from the Tuebingen theologians and the Stuttgart consistory and then sent them directly to Duke Julius with a covering letter which flattered the duke as being the prince most zealously furthering the concordistic activity and himself as being a theologian who knew no guile. Julius, of course, was pleased, and he commissioned Chemnitz to round up support for Andreae's articles.

Though in general the approval was forthcoming, yet in specific instances so many suggestions for revision were being made that Chytraeus ended up rewriting two of the articles completely, the second on Free Will and the seventh on the Lord's Supper, and the entire proposal underwent a thorough revision at the hand of Chemnitz.[61] When this "Swabian-Saxon Concord" (1575) was returned to Andreae, he had difficulty recognizing it as the work he had sent out for approval. As a matter of fact it was no longer his work and had it not been for his tremendous self-control he would have responded in anger. But he accepted the move, presumably because it still recognized him as the leading figure in the concordistic attempt and because for him the goal was not so much to see his own formulation of the dogma in print as it was to experience the day when unity was restored to Lutheranism.[62]

Still this would never have occurred had Andreae not opportunely found another prince who placed confidence in him as a true "servant of the Lord."[63] Elector August of Albertine Saxony had been serving as guardian of the Ernestine princes and as such had unwittingly tolerated Philippism. In 1573 he cracked down hard on the Gnesio-Lutheran obstructionists to religious peace at Jena.[64] However, the following year he did the same against the extreme wing of the left, the Philippists at Wittenberg, and thus he created a favorable climate for the type of activity which Andreae had in mind.

As a continuing means of testing the orthodoxy of his theologians, August felt the need for a formula of orthodox doctrine. Two Wuerttembergian theologians, Lucas Osiander and Balthasar Bidembach, had been asked to provide such a formula. Though Andreae was not officially involved in this task, perhaps because of his earlier reputation as a theologian of exchange rather than of exclusion, it is quite inconceivable that he did not influence it from behind the scenes.[65] At any rate the new document, known as the "Maulbronn Formula," was forwarded to August about the same time that he received a copy of the "Swabian-Saxon Concord" (1576) and thus the elector was confronted with a choice. To help him make the decision he called upon the by now well-known Andreae, and there was none more willing to oblige.

It was most likely not the purest of motives which prompted Andreae to recommend the "Maulbronn Formula" as the preferable of the two documents. He said that whereas the "Swabian-Saxon Concord" lacked the smooth style of a single author and made excessive use of technical terminology, the "Maulbronn Formula" was crystal clear, easy to comprehend, and used the terminology of Scripture and the earlier confessions. Was this not perhaps Andreae's way of repaying Chemnitz and Chytraeus in kind for the treatment they had given his original "Swabian Concordia"? Be that as it may, Andreae convinced August of the need to call in some "safe theologians" such as Chemnitz and Chytraeus, not to mention himself, who would conflate the two documents now in hand.

The meeting took place at Torgau, some 30 miles southeast of Wittenberg, beginning in May of 1576.[66] Andreae at this time enjoyed the support of Selnecker, and both of them were looked upon as the trusted representatives of August. Nevertheless under the influence of Chemnitz and Chytraeus and the support given them by Musculus and Koerner, the "Maulbronn Formula" was relegated to secondary importance at Torgau, the "Swabian-Saxon Concord" serving as the basic text while improvements were then made in keeping with certain of the advantages recognized as belonging to the "Maulbronn Formula." The "Torgau Book," as this reworking was called, contained the 12 articles of the later recension known as the Formula of Concord, and in the same sequence. A service of thanksgiving, with Selnecker delivering the sermon, marked the happy termination and favorable outcome of the discussions. Andreae wrote in a letter to Heshusius and Wigand: "Often were they [Chemnitz and Chytraeus] almost overwhelmed with rejoicing and wonder that we were there [at Torgau] brought to such deliberation. Truly, this is the change of the right hand of the Most High. . . ."[67]

The elector now saw the accomplishment of a concord as something for which he could be credited, so he commissioned Andreae to obtain signatures for the "Torgau Book." To Andreae's surprise he still met with a good deal of opposition. In Hesse, for example, the authors of the "Torgau Book" were accused of trying to improve on the Word of God. But Andreae carried on with the determination of one who could smell victory just ahead. He advised against holding a general synod as the means of obtaining final approval for the "Torgau Book," at least not before the many critiques had been considered by a committee of theologians and the necessary changes incorporated in it. August agreed, and the "Big Three," Andreae, Chemnitz, and Selnecker, met at Bergen Abbey in March of 1577 to follow this course.

In response to the criticism of wordiness, Andreae with apparent relish shortened the articles on Free Will and the Lord's Supper. Chytraeus, who had authored these articles, was later to bemoan what Andreae had done to his work in his absence.[68] Andreae also assumed the task of providing a summary version (Epitome) of the entire document, which was not to replace the original but to precede it, that those Lutherans who run might also read.[69] To please the Gnesio-Lutherans, who felt the expression "that some theologians had strayed away from some of the articles of the Augsburg Confession" was to put it mildly, the words were substituted that they "had strayed extremely far away from some central and important articles."[70]

Since these changes and many more of a similar nature were bound to raise antagonisms on one side or the other, which then at a general synod would be debated until no one again could leave as victor but instead all would end up condemning each other and the last state of confused Lutheranism would be worse than the first (which had been exposed at Worms in 1557), Andreae determined to prevent such a synod.[71] This required unlimited tact lest by his fears he himself betray the continued disunity of Lutheranism—disunity because even though theological unity might be achieved on paper, the psychological disunity which had both accompanied and followed the theological disunity could not be healed so quickly. So Andreae met unofficially with Chemnitz and Selnecker, shared his fears, and won their approval for attempting a revision which would gain general approval without the procedure of ratification by a general synod. To this end a second official meeting was to be held at Bergen Abbey, with the size of the revising committee being doubled so that it now included most of the team that had worked on the "Torgau Book."[72] Thus also all the territories most strongly inclined toward Lutheranism would be represented: Andreae from Wuerttemberg, Chemnitz from Brunswick, Selnecker from Saxony, Chytraeus from Mecklenburg, and Musculus and Koerner from Brandenburg.

This meeting at Bergen Abbey (near Magdeburg) took place in May of 1577. As Andreae conceived of it, its purpose was not a final, rigorous revision of the "Torgau Book" on the basis of the written critiques which had been submitted, but rather a confirmation by the enlarged and more representative committee of the changes already made by the triumvirate. This then was to be followed by a signature-assembling campaign which would be all the easier if each member of the committee of six first affixed his own signature without qualification. Andreae managed to engineer this feat with only Chytraeus giving him any amount of resistance.[73] On May 28, 1577, the revised form of the "Torgau Book" was submitted to Elector August. Known as the "Bergic Book" or the Formula of Concord, its formulation was an indication of the success which Andreae's new policy of exclusion, i. e., exlusion of the extremists by means of antitheses with accompanying condemnations, was able to effect.

3) Concordia Through Expulsion (1577—90)

"If anyone abhors the Formula of Concord or thinks it contains errors, he has no idea what it's all about."[74] In making this judgment about his labor of love, Andreae was probably closer to the truth than he himself realized. No one who adequately appreciated the need for Lutheran unity, who sufficiently recognized the myriad obstacles standing in its way, and who was certain that "our competence is from God, who has made us competent to be ministers of a new covenant, not in a written code but in the Spirit" (2 Cor. 3:5 f.)—no one who understood all this could simply write the Formula of Concord off as a detestable work of man attempting to do what only God can do. That the Formula was a work of man has become clear enough in this study of the

41

life of Jakob Andreae, but it should also have become clear that this man understood himself to be and was a "servant of the Lord."

But perhaps neither Andreae nor his critics understood well enough that "the Lord is the Spirit, and where the Spirit of the Lord is, there is freedom" (2 Cor. 3:17). Concordia through *exchange* had failed because of the sinfulness of men. Concordia through *exclusion* was a realistic and necessary recognition of the imperfection of sinful men. But concordia through *expulsion* was to fail to recognize the source of the church's sufficiency and to exchange the Spirit's gift of the freedom to love for the Old Evil Foe's bondage of hate whereby, to borrow an idea from the Formula of Concord itself, the *distinction* between substance and accident is instead translated into *separation* and the "weak brother" is simply gotten off our back. [75]

Expulsion of the brother who would not sign the Formula of Concord—that was the final stage in Andreae's life, the stage which presents him more as a servant of the secular ruler to whom the sword was given than as a servant of the Lord who, when He is "lifted up from the earth, will draw all men to [Himself]" (John 12:32). [76]

Andreae spent the three years after the historic meetings at Bergen Abbey using all means at his disposal to gain support for the Formula of Concord and its implementation as the law of the land. His patron, Elector August, had declared: "By the help of God I am determined, as long as I live, to keep my churches and schools pure and in agreement with the Formula of Concord. Whoever does not want to cooperate with me may go; I have no desire for him. God protect me, and those belonging to me, from papists and Calvinists—I have experienced it." [77] There is no doubt that the Peace of Augsburg was on August's side, but it is another question whether the conduct called for by that peace is the most that could and should be required of a Christian. Andreae and the entire generation of Lutherans surrounding the origin of the Formula of Concord spoke the prophetic Word to the princes of their day for the most part only insofar as it did not contradict the prevailing stage of cultural development. They were thoroughly rooted in their own history, and the revelatory Word was applied to it not to abolish it but to perfect it. [78]

It has been correctly stated that some territorial rulers and theologians refused to append their names to the Formula of Concord for political reasons. [79] What these same historians neglect to emphasize with equal clarity, however, is that there were also good political reasons *for* signing the Formula of Concord. This document is inextricably tied to what one historian has called, in contrast to the *reformatio ecclesiastica* before 1555, the *reformatio in politicis* after 1555.[80] Most of Andreae's ministry fell into this latter period.

The expulsion of the recalcitrant, of course, did not take place at the point of the sword. This was unnecessary since suspension from office and retention of salary had the same effect.[81] The "religious seriousness and moral determination" exhibited here by Andreae and others is worthy of imitation, but the means used to express these ought not be above criticism. There is something suspicious about a confessional policy which produces more martyrs among the objectors to a confession than among the confessors.[82]

A variation on the expulsion theme was played by Andreae in connection with the preparation of a Preface for *The Book of Concord*.[83] When it became clear to him that the objections being registered against the Formula of Concord could not be satisfactorily handled by changes in the text or by simply disregarding them, he reverted to the diplomatic tactics of his earlier years, more certain of their success now since the "exchanges" being suggested were set in the larger context of "expulsion." It was a matter of finding a way of satisfying vested interests on various sides of an issue or of the weaker party being expelled.

By way of example, the vested interest of the Lower Saxons in striking out the word "Christian" as an accurate description of the Frankfurt Recess (1558) and the Naumburg Assembly (1561) had to be balanced out against another vested interest, that of Elector Ludwig of the Palatinate, who wished that word included lest his deceased father, Frederick III, by its omission be declared a heretic. The compromise description of these events as being "well-intended" (if not Christian!) had, in turn, to be balanced out against still another vested interest, this one surrounding Duke Julius of Brunswick. He had blown his high standing in the minds of the Lutheran princes and theologians in 1578 by permitting his 14-year-old son to be consecrated bishop of Halberstadt with Roman Catholic rites, an act more political than religious but certainly not one which could be considered an adiaphoron.[84] For this confessional betrayal Chemnitz had highly and publicly criticized him, but now when as a result he threatened to withhold his signature from the Formula of Concord, Andreae humored him with promises to meet certain of his demands, among them the striking even of the epithet "well-intended." By doing so Andreae seemed permanently to have damaged his own relationship with Chemnitz as he disclosed himself once again to be a "flexible" man. He was this, of course, but (as he thought) only insofar as he might thereby be all the more a "servant of the Lord" (cf. 2 Cor. 8:19-23).

The Formula of Concord was finally published with great to-do in connection with the Dresden trade exposition on June 25, 1580, exactly 50 years after the Augsburg Confession had been presented to Emperor Charles V. But the event was to become a bittersweet victory for Andreae, who more than any other person had made it possible. The stress and strain of so much wheeling and dealing had left Andreae more belligerent than was his wont, and few there were in Germany who wished to call him their friend—certainly Chemnitz, Chytraeus, and Selnecker did not. Nor did Elector August.

The story of Andreae's release from his duties in Saxony is not a pleasant one. Just when it might be expected that he would be riding the crest of his popularity, everyone seemed to have turned against his person, even Elector August, whose explicit confidence he had held for close to five years. Though officially released with honor and bearing gifts (e. g., a gilded cup and a Complutensian Polyglot Bible presented with the words "to the very honorable restorer of the heavenly doctrine, deserving of the highest praise from the church of Christ" and inscribed by August's own hand with the words "at last the good triumphs"),[85] behind all the court protocol, retained for the sake of the success of the cause itself, another mood nevertheless prevailed. Andreae's erstwhile friend Selnecker changed his mind about him and began to keep an uncomplimentary log on his activities.[86] This was enough to shatter the elector's trust in him, so much so that he refused to see him in strict privacy again and required that promises drawn from him be put in writing and signed.[87]

Fortunately for Andreae the last 10 years of his life after his return to Tuebingen were so filled with activity that he was forced to carry on with his accustomed enthusiasm without extended whimpering about the treatment accorded him at his departure from Saxony. However, he never moved beyond his expulsionist stance, which is not surprising since confessional/evangelical tolerance was to be a gift of God to a later generation. This is a gift which Lutherans about to celebrate the 400th anniversary of the Formula and *Book of Concord* are still struggling to receive since to this date the tension between a confessional/evangelical stance and one which is merely tolerant has generally been resolved so as to betray the one or the other.

Death came to Andreae in Tuebingen at the age of 61 years after a 21-day siege of pleurisy. On the day before his death he called the rector of the university and a number of the ruling clergy of the city to his home to hear and witness his final public confession. In the context of a confession of his sins and the reception of the Lord's Supper he said:

> Now you are all well aware of what has been my teaching in matters dealing with the faith, as I have publicly presented it both in churches and in schools, at home and abroad, in sermons and books throughout these 44 years of my ministry. By this teaching I abide, and when my God and Lord takes me out of this world, I desire to depart this life, with the help of God, standing by this confession, and on the basis of his holy Word to defend and give account of the same before the judgment throne of Jesus Christ on the last day. As a testimony thereto I now desire to receive the true body and the true blood of Christ, my Redeemer. Of this my confession I desire that you give witness for me before the entire world, and should slanderous rumors be spread concerning me to deny them before the church on the basis of my present action. [88]

Most encyclopedia articles conclude by characterizing Jakob Andreae somewhat as the following: " . . . Andreae emerges as self-assured and self-willed, frequently tactless and overbearing, all too often imprudent in his choice of words; at the same time he was deeply pious, conscious of his own faults, endlessly diligent and industrious, a powerful preacher, an eminently practical theologian, and a tenaciously and honestly devoted proponent of Lutheran unity."[89] His epitaph included the word *fidelissimus,* i. e., "ever faithful."[90] And that he was: faithful to the notion that one must confess, faithful against libertarian enthusiasm, faithful to his secular lords, and above all faithful to the Lord of lords—not by being without sin but by living and dying in the forgiveness of sins through his Lord Jesus Christ. Like his Biblical namesake he was tricky—but all for the sake of the promise.

MARTIN CHEMNITZ
—THE CONFESSOR?

St. Martin (d. 397), Bishop of Tours and Confessor, is remembered by the church particularly on his feast day, the 11th of November. Two of his namesakes, Martin Luther and Martin Chemnitz, have given that day added significance for those happening to have a penchant for the development of a Lutheran hagiography. No such persons would haggle too long as to the propriety of Luther's inclusion in such a study, for what Lutheran isn't impressed by the gift God has given the church in Martin Luther? The inclusion of Martin Chemnitz, however, might call for a greater degree of the gift of the discernment of spirits. What might be perfectly obvious to some Lutherans might appear considerably less so to others. The question will be clearly decided in Chemnitz' favor when the sole criterion for the decision is Jesus Christ and not Martin Luther. Chemnitz' faithfulness to Luther will be debated as long as theologians consider the question important. His faithfulness as a confessor of Jesus as Lord is more easily demonstrated. Thus Luther himself would cast his vote unhesitatingly in favor of Chemnitz.

Martin Chemnitz was born on Nov. 9, 1522, at Treuenbrietzen, about 20 miles north-northeast of Wittenberg. In his autobiography he characteristically writes: ". . . when I pursued mathematical studies, by comparison with certain events I figured out that my birth had taken place . . . at 47 minutes after 12 p.m."[1] His father's name was Paul, and he was a weaver and merchant despite the fact that he came from an old and wealthy noble family, whose name, Chemnitz, meant "von Stein." The above-mentioned Lutheran hagiographers might detect in this a parallel to Jesus' word about "rock," spoken in response to Peter's confession. His mother's maiden name was Koldeborn; her Christian name, interestingly, Euphemia, the Greek for "prayer and praise," which are also forms of confession. Even the name of his birthplace, Treuenbrietzen, betrays an element of confessional faithfulness, as Chemnitz himself calls to our attention in his autobiography.[2] Martin was the third of three children born to Paul and Euphemia. Although he lost his father in death when only 11 years old, he did not seem to lack a mother's love, for he writes: ". . . my mother reposed great hopes in me and loved me more than her remaining children, who were, for this reason, not well disposed toward me."[3]

If the day and place of Chemnitz' birth seemed to portend something as to his future, so also did the year, 1522. It was the year in which Luther cut short his "exile" at the Wartburg in order to return to Wittenberg in the hope of saving a reformation which was quickly turning into a revolution at the hands of Carlstadt and Zwilling. The "second Martin" too would one day have to cut short his happy exile as librarian in the duke's castle to meet the violent disturbances resulting from the theological views of Osiander and others and serve there where he could restore, as Luther once did, an uneasy peace in the "Lutheran household." So as was the case with the man who was later to become his co-worker in the restoration of this peace, Jakob Andreae, the child was indeed father of the man.

The Child

Already as a youngster Martin gave evidence of that genius which he would one day place at the disposal of his beloved Lutheran Church. He tended to be a loner, preferring to be isolated with his thoughts to playing in company with the other children in the streets. An accident as a child once frightened him to such an extent that he began to stammer and stutter and to walk in his sleep, but he outgrew it after three or four years, as he did also the ability of his teacher at Treuenbrietzen to cultivate his talents.[4] So he made his first pilgrimage to Wittenberg, where at age 14 (1536) he attended the elementary school. His experience at the school was rather negative, but he nevertheless later recalled that during those short six months in Wittenberg "it gave me pleasure to see excellent people and hear Luther when he preached." But his family didn't think it worth the expense.[5]

Meanwhile the situation in Treuenbrietzen hadn't improved, so in 1538 he was compelled to leave school and to lend his brother a hand at the cloth-making trade, his brother having complained that it was not fair that he should work while Martin consumed.[6] Though the apostle Paul was able to make a go of tent-making, cloth-making was not Martin's thing and he pleaded to be allowed to return to school; but, he writes, "the answer was ever the same: It costs too much."[7] At last a relative was persuaded to take his part, and as a result he was able to attend an excellent school at Magdeburg, 60 miles west of Treuenbrietzen, from 1539 to 1542. There he was instructed in Latin and Greek, dialectics, rhetoric, and to his particular delight, the principles of astronomy. But his family balked at the expense of continuing his education at a university, so he was forced to take on a position as tutor at Calbe, some 20 miles to the south of Magdeburg, where he served successfully for about four months. Then he took his meager savings, added to it what little his mother had given him, and matriculated (1543) at the University of Frankfurt/Oder, for Martin a long 130 miles to the east of Magdeburg. A relative of his through his mother was professor there, a certain Georg Sabinus, a son-in-law of Melanchthon. But before a year had passed his financial resources were again exhausted and he took a position as schoolmaster at nearby Wriezen. Here he remained a year and a half (1544—45) and studiously read the books he had learned to value during his brief stay at the university. When once again his savings allowed it, he quit his position and pilgrimaged a second time to Wittenberg (1545), this time to study at the feet of Melanchthon and others at the University. At Melanchthon's advice he devoted himself to mathematics and delighted also in the study of astrology.[8] As a bonus he heard Luther lecture, preach, and conduct his last disputation, but by his own admission he "did not hear him with due attention then."[9]

Again his studies were interrupted—this time by the unsettling effects of the Smalcald War. When in 1547 Duke John Frederick lost the city of Wittenberg to Maurice, he also lost the university, so Chemnitz sought a more congenial atmosphere far to the north at Koenigsberg in East Prussia.[10] Here he tutored some young Polish noblemen, plied his astrological avocation, and finally a year later became rector of the Kneiphof school at Koenigsberg. Encouraged and assisted by his relative Sabinus, who was now rector of the new university established there by Duke Albrecht, he took his master's degree there in 1548, the duke bearing all the expenses. The duke was attracted to the now 26-year-old Chemnitz by the latter's publication of a German almanac or calendar and by his astrological predictions.[11] In his autobiography Chemnitz admits that he himself was uncertain about "the foundation for such predictions" but that he wished to make use of it only "to scrape together thereby the necessary means for other studies."[12] Which "other studies"? In a letter written to Melanchthon about this time Chemnitz asked him for "a method of properly instituting and shaping the study of theology," to which Melanchthon among other things replied "that the chief light and best method in theological study was to observe the difference between the Law and the Gospel."[13] One would hesitate to accuse Chemnitz of employing astrology according to the principle employed by his worst adversaries, the Jesuits (viz., "the end justifies the means"), but his subsequent thoughts on the question of adiaphora might prompt us to wonder about the "boldness" of Chemnitz' "confession" at this early point in his life.

If Chemnitz revealed a weakness here, it was soon to be overshadowed, if not excused, by subsequent events. On April 5, 1550, the 27-year-old Chemnitz was given the appointment as librarian of the ducal castle library, an event of which he writes: "I look upon this as the greatest fortune God bestowed upon me during the time of my studies."[14] At last he had the books and the circumstances he needed to pursue his education in a systematic, even though largely independent, way. He quickly dropped notions of studying medicine or jurisprudence and devoted himself entirely to theology, a subject which had always interested him for personal and devotional reasons. This turn of events he could thankfully ascribe to "God governing my course."[15]

God's initial training period for this "confessor" was now finally and rapidly coming to a close. It was a training quite different from that given the "first Martin," who was dramatically and existentially purified in a crucible marked with the sign of the cross of Christ. The "second Martin's" purification occurred when the rainbow he had been following since his first pilgrimage to Wittenberg ended with a pot of literary gold at the ducal library in Koenigsberg.[16] He was now thirty years old and the evidence was about to burst forth that also in his case the child was father of the man.

The Father

During his three-year (1550—53) period of self-instruction in the ducal "seminary" library Chemnitz followed a definite method: exegesis and isagogics, church history, dogmatics and apologetics. All his reading was accompanied by copious note-taking, notes which in 1570 he writes "I still have and often consult with great delight and profit."[17] While Chemnitz was intently pursuing his theological studies in the ducal library, theological controversies were raging just outside. Andrew Osiander (1498—1552) touched off the spark when after resigning his post in Nuernberg because of the introduction of the Interim (1548) he moved to Koenigsberg, where he was enthusiastically received by Duke Albrecht, whom he had gained for the Reformation about 25 years before. Early in 1549 the duke appointed him pastor of the Old City Church and, soon thereafter, ranking professor of theology at the University of Koenigsberg, with a double salary. Already in his inaugural disputation he hinted at his "deviant" views on justification, and by 1551 the fires of controversy were raging almost uncontrollably. [18] Joachim Moerlin (1514—71), soon thereafter to become Chemnitz' closest friend, attacked Osiander publicly from his pulpit at the cathedral in Koenigsberg. Various synods as well as individual theologians submitted their opinions on the controversy during 1551—52. Just about the time the matter was coming to a climax, however, Osiander died (1552). The duke then enjoined silence on both parties and Moerlin was banished. From Brunswick, where he had accepted a position as superintendent, Moerlin continued zealously to extinguish every spark of Osiandrism. [19]—But what has all this to do with our secluded "seminarian-librarian"?

In 1550 Chemnitz, together with a second theologian, was designated by the duke to oppose Osiander at a public disputation. Chemnitz' bold assault on the ducal favorite almost resulted in his own dismissal, Chemnitz claiming that "next to God I had my one protection in my astrology, without which the duke would not do." [20] Thus he was caught in a conflict of loyalties, to his friend Moerlin and to his ducal benefactor, a circumstance which prompted Chemnitz to resign his post at the end of 1552. [21] The duke tried to retain him for the sake of his horoscopes. He therefore, as Chemnitz writes, "offered to give me a decent annual stipend *ad studia,* if I would oblige myself to serve him before others." [22] But Chemnitz had no desire to be "obliged" to any court, so he took his leave from Prussia in the spring of 1553 with "200 thalers *ad studia"* in a promissory note which the duke had given "without obligation, only that I should cast a few horoscopes every year for His Grace." [23] Thus Chemnitz carried through his first public confessional stand.

With this new event entered into his *curriculum vitae* and with a letter of recommendation from Sabinus in hand, Chemnitz made his third pilgrimage to Wittenberg. Melanchthon meanwhile had inherited Luther's authoritative position at Wittenberg (opposed by Flacius at Jena), and Chemnitz now became a boarder in Melanchthon's home and his attentive student.[24] In January of 1554 he was admitted to the philosophical faculty as an examiner, and by June he accepted Melanchthon's invitation to lecture on the latter's *Loci communes.* His large student audiences were a testimony to Chemnitz' effectiveness as a teacher. Much to the disappointment of all at Wittenberg, Chemnitz soon accepted a call as preacher at the St. Aegidienkirche and as coadjutor to the superintendent at Brunswick, his recently made friend and co-confessor at Koenigsberg, Moerlin.[25] In spite of the prospect of achieving academic fame at Wittenberg, Chemnitz was probably attracted by the possibility of being rejoined to his friend Moerlin and by the more directly pastoral duties of preacher and coadjutor. Perhaps he also already had a premonition from the stars that Melanchthon's Wittenberg and he were on a collision course.[26]

On Nov. 25, 1554, John Bugenhagen (1485—1558), the original developer of the Reformation in Brunswick (1528), ordained Chemnitz to the sacred ministry, and five days later Chemnitz bade farewell to Wittenberg and his honored teacher Melanchthon.[27] On Dec. 15, 1554, he was invested with his new office in Brunswick, the city which he continued to serve faithfully in spiritual matters until the end of his life. In August of 1555 he married Anna, daughter of Hermann Jaeger, licentiate of laws. Anna, described as "devout, beautiful, and thrifty," bore him three sons and seven daughters, of whom one son and three daughters preceded him in death.[28] His family life is described as having been a thoroughly happy one, compensating somewhat for the many trials which would accompany his professional career.[29]

Brunswick developed early as a mighty fortress of Lutheranism. Bugenhagen was impressed already in 1528 with the manner in which the congregational reform there was geared into the body politic, "so that the former penetrated the latter and the freedom guaranteed by the civic constitution carried over into the ecclesiastical organization."[30] A prime factor in the arrangement was the so-called "Colloquium," a meeting of the entire body of local clergy held every two weeks at which all church-related questions were openly discussed and a consensus sought. Any additional sectarianlike coteries were strictly forbidden. Thus an amazing unanimity was achieved in questions dealing with doctrine, ritual, worship, and discipline.[31] And to achieving such unanimity Moerlin and his friend, the new coadjutor, confessed a firm commitment, the former pursuing a role "similar" to that of Luther, the latter to that of Melanchthon.[32]

The year 1557 found the two friends involved in relieving the tensions evoked by the Adiaphoristic and Synergistic Controversies. That same year they attended the famous Colloquy at Worms, from which Moerlin, together with other right-wingers, was eventually pressured to exclude himself and of which Chemnitz felt that the trip wasn't worth the effort except for the fact that he became acquainted with some of the leading theologians of the day, especially those of South Germany.[33]

At home in Brunswick Chemnitz was busy with semiannual public disputations on a selected set of doctrinal theses, with regular weekly lectures in Latin on Melanchthon's *Loci*, with the study of Hebrew (the language first used by God, as he believed) and, of course, with an abundance of preaching. At first his preaching effectiveness lagged behind that of the fiery Moerlin, but slowly he developed a style which engaged the attention of large audiences. His approach was simple and emphatic, not so much dogmatically as Biblically structured, more pedagogically oriented than evangelistic, polemical but this with evangelical moderation, and always directed to the conscience. The following example, taken from a sermon preached on New Year's Day, is not only entertaining but highly instructive even 400 years later:

> It is not an evil custom to wish someone a Christian, joyful, and blessed New Year, a holiday already observed by the heathen. Celebrated also among the papists, it was customary to announce the New Year's blessing from the pulpit, which practice originally stemmed from good intentions but later fell into abuse when the monks began pulling tricks and thereby provoked laughter in the churches. Neither is it a bad idea to follow the custom whereby the New Year greeting is shared with the various social classes by giving each a distinctively representative animal. The preachers were given a dove on New Year's Day in order to show that like the dove which Noah released from the ark, preachers too should witness to us in their sermons of the grace and mercy of God in Christ. Governmental officials were given a pelikan, a bird which rather than permit its young to perish will tear open its breast and let its own blood gush forth over its young that they might again be thereby warmed and revived; this is to symbolize the fact that it is the duty of the government to be prepared to shed its blood for its subjects—*pro lege et grege* (for the law and for the people). Fathers and mothers were given an ant, which Solomon says is so industrious and solicitous during the summer and autumn that it drags together food particles into its hill in order that it might be well supplied

throughout the winter when nothing is to be found in the fields; thus the head of a family is also to see to it that he always has enough for himself and his family. Servants and subordinates are given a bee, which characteristically have only one king or leader and thus all hold to him and recognize him alone as their lord and master; so also all domestic servants and subordinates ought to honor their king and lord and to hold him in respect. Finally, women and maidens are given a snail, which at all times carries its little house with it in order to crawl into it; just so it is best that the female sex stay close to home and not run around outside of it.[34]

Thus Chemnitz attempted to reach the conscience of each of his parishioners. But he also directed his attention to instruction at a more formally academic level. Together with the superintendent he was obliged to hold theological lectures for the educated. Already in 1555 he began his series of lectures on Melanchthon's *Loci communes*. He demonstrated his sovereignty over the wealth of historical sources upon which he drew by not dictating his lectures but rather developing them in a spontaneous manner. These were published as the *Loci theologici* only after his death by Polycarp Leyser in 1591. A present-day scholar and admirer of Chemnitz writes of them:

> The work resembles a Biblical theology as much as a dogmatics; it contains many lengthy and pertinent word studies of significant Biblical themes such as faith, grace, and justification, and it offers several very thorough exegeses of pericopes relevant to Baptism, the Lord's Supper, the Trinity, and the like. There are also allusions to history and to the development of dogmas in the church, and there are some rather long discussions of ecclesiastical terms. . . . But essentially we have in this enormous book a systematic presentation of Biblical theology. . . . Large as it is, the *Loci theologici* makes enjoyable reading.[35]

As coadjutor Chemnitz supported Moerlin's attempt to sustain the practice of church discipline (*excommunicatio minor*—exclusion from the Sacrament), which they carefully distinguished from the ban (*excommunicatio major*—civil exile). The latter was strictly a function of the state and was not to be confused with the former, which was the presupposition for the latter. For instance, a burgher by the name of Henning Klod was suspected of Zwinglianism. He was barred from the Sacrament and later when he desired to marry, his request was denied him until he should admit and confess his error. A period of time followed during which attempts were made to reach agreement. When these failed, however, the city council unanimously condemned him as a Sacramentarian and he was banished from the city. He lived for four years in Wittenberg, after which he finally admitted and confessed his error, asked that he be prayed for from the pulpit, that God forgive him, and that he again be received as a brother into the congregation.[36] Thus the whole banishment question hinged on the preceding question of the man's excommunication from the Sacrament.

In 1561 Chemnitz became involved in the Hardenberg case. Hardenberg was preacher at the cathedral in Bremen, where he entertained views of the Sacrament that were considered Calvinistic. At a meeting of the district representatives held in Brunswick in 1561 Hardenberg was declared "a despiser of the Augsburg Confession, Sacramentarian, disturber of the peace, and incorrigible false teacher," who therefore had to be dismissed from his office. Although Chemnitz had not taken part in the proceedings, he had been given an opportunity to review Hardenberg's confession, and in response to this he submitted a written opinion in which he exposed Hardenberg's Calvinistic line of reasoning and demonstrated by means of historical arguments the necessity of interpreting Article X of the Augsburg Confession in Luther's sense.[37] What Chemnitz found particularly disturbing was the apparent dishonesty in the word-games played by the Crypto-Calvinists. Whereas Zwingli and his followers had not been deceitful, the present-day sacramentarians concealed their error with ambiguous, deceptive words.[38]

That same year there appeared Chemnitz' first theological publication, a lengthy treatise on the Lord's Supper. He emphasized the interpretation of the Words of Institution as opposed to Christological speculation and the importance of distinguishing questions having to do with the substance and essence of the Sacrament from those dealing only with its power and effect. He found Calvinists more interested in the latter questions than the former, and this tended to be the great weakness of their approach. He felt, however, that the controversies about the ubiquity of Christ's humanity needlessly confused the issue as well as consciences.[39]

Moerlin's "Lueneburg Articles" also appeared in 1561 as his answer to what he considered the spineless confession made by the princes at Naumburg earlier that year, spineless because it included no specific condemnation of the false teachings then disturbing the Lutheran

Church.[40] Chemnitz and other theologians signed these articles, but he could not refrain from warning that one should not overlook the "difference between necessary controversies and those which arrogance and party hatred had provoked."[41] On this occasion and others Chemnitz felt obliged to speak a restraining word to his overzealous friend.[42]

The following year Chemnitz became involved in the long controversy with the Jesuits and the Roman Catholic Church that was to engage almost all his leisure for nearly a decade.[43] In the creeping success of the Jesuit Order to undermine the Reformation he saw a very real threat, and he rose to meet it hardly aware that he was like a David going forth to confess God's honor before an enemy boasting a new Goliathlike hero, the Decrees of the Council of Trent.[44] In Koeln the Jesuits were in control of the theological faculty and in 1560 had taken occasion at the publication of a Protestant catechism written by John Monhemius, headmaster of the academy at nearby Duesseldorf, to respond with a *Censura* intended to praise the glory of the Roman Catholic Church and to put the Protestants in their place. This prompted Chemnitz to enter the lists in 1562 with his "The Chief Chapter of the Theology of the Jesuits, Taken from an Evaluation of Theirs and Annotated." It has been characterized by a contemporary scholar as follows:

> The sharp, sometimes witty, sometimes heavily ironic, but consistently hard-hitting attack on the Neopelagianism and the indefensible hermeneutics of the *Censura* takes the position that the Jesuit doctrine represents a new development within the papalist community which deserves a specific refutation.[45]

Chemnitz burnt sensitive Jesuit flesh with his book, and the counterfire began promptly. After a completely incompetent opponent attempted to answer him, a Portuguese university professor, James Payva d'Andrada (1528—76?), took up the gauntlet. He apparently chanced on Chemnitz' book while still attending the Council of Trent, and thus he answered Chemnitz with its decrees still ringing in his ears. No slouch, the Jesuit professor's reply added up to a 10-book work with a rigidly authoritarian viewpoint such as was characteristic of the Iberian bishops attending the council. Could the coadjutor from Brunswick continue against this Goliathan work with just a sling and five smooth stones?

Even this Lutheran "David" had to gulp at the stature of his opponent, and his interpreters will long debate whether he stuck to sling and stones or whether he ran back for reinforcement and a second go at it with Saul's armor. [46] Whatever the case may be, by the time Chemnitz had completed his *Examen concilii Tridentini,* [47] it must have appeared to his "Philistine" opponents like Michelangelo's towering, powerful "David." Reinhard Mumm, the author of the most definitive study of the *Examen,* writes:

> Compared with Luther and Melanchthon, Chemnitz is altogether epigone; within the circle of epigones Flacius excelled him as an academician and Brenz as a more thorough digester of Luther's world of thought. Nevertheless as the chief author of the Formula of Concord, the creator of the *Examen,* and of the first major Lutheran dogmatics Chemnitz remains the most influential of all of Luther's disciples. [48]

Is it any wonder, then, that already in 1566 Duke Albrecht of Prussia tried to reenlist both Moerlin and Chemnitz to calm his theologically troubled land through the reorganization of its church?

Chemnitz had received similar invitations from Halle and Goettingen but at the urging of the Brunswick city council turned them down. Albrecht had to extend his invitation twice before the council reluctantly granted its two heroes a three-month leave of absence, beginning in the spring of 1567, in order that they might assist the aging and repentant duke with the rereformation of his land. They immediately set to work preparing a *corpus doctrinae* which would invalidate the Philippistic norm established through the influence of Matthew Vogel and John Funk in 1558. The "new" *Corpus doctrinae Pruthenicum* consisted of the Augsburg Confession and its Apology, the Smalcald Articles, and 10 articles composed by Chemnitz which dealt with doctrinal deviations and the responsibility of the bishops, ecclesiastical dignitaries, and university professors to implement the new norm. [49] By June of 1567 this norm became law and Chemnitz and Moerlin were ready to return to Brunswick, though the duke exerted much pressure to retain them.

A few weeks later an impressive delegation from Duke Albrecht arrived in Brunswick with instructions not to leave unless they were bringing Moerlin and Chemnitz with them. The entire citizenry became involved in the following two weeks of negotiations. Finally the council agreed to release Moerlin if Chemnitz would remain and become his successor as superintendent. Chemnitz wrestled mightily with his calls and asked the clergy to commend the matter to their parishioners for prayer. When pressed for a decision he declared:

Although previously I could not but now have learned to recognize that the call is legitimate and a proper declaration of the divine will, and since I have not thought it right to omit the third petition of the Lord's Prayer nor to appear overly clear-sighted before our Lord God in reference to my calls, I accordingly forthwith announced it publicly because all of us are desirous that this turn out propitiously. And should we now wish to have a manifestation of the divine will, necessity would demand that we would mutually indicate that we are such as would gladly see and desire that this matter be instigated, conducted, and completed according to God's Word, command, and will. Then we could in truth say that it was begun in God's name and we could all the more joyfully comfort ourselves that God, who is faithful and good, would be present among us with His Spirit, blessing us with all His gifts. [50]

The "manifestation of the divine will" Chemnitz proposed to see in the willingness of the ministerium and the city council to accept the conditions he would now lay before them. If they for their part were willing to accept his provisos, he for his part would be willing to serve as their superintendent. Among the conditions he proposed were the following:

In reference to the ministerium—

1. that they not only preach and teach affirmatively with one mind, heart, and mouth in accordance with the *corpus doctrinae,* but that they also unitedly and consistently in necessary controversies oppose all deviations;

2. that the Colloquium should be maintained and regularly attended by all the pastors, for it alone should constitute the forum for the discussion of all questions relating to the pastoral office;

3. that the superintendent should not be esteemed for his person but for his office, which was incapable of being fulfilled if the brethren did not accord the superintendent the required honor and obedience.

In reference to the city council—

1. that it not interfere with the pastors as they carry out their obligations in accordance with the *corpus doctrinae;*

2. that it recognize not only the teaching office of the pastors but also their disciplinary office, for God at all times assigned prophets to the kings who were from God's Word to admonish and discipline the government as to its responsibility;

3. that it not interfere with the execution of church discipline but help to further it and to this purpose establish a consistory whose responsibility should not be confused with that of the government;

4. that it respect and maintain the institution of the Colloquium, referring all its ecclesiastical concerns to it;

5. that it leave the supervision of Christian schools, since they are a function of the church, to the superintendent and the Colloquium, who are also responsible for the approval and hiring of school personnel;

6. that it not undertake the calling of a coadjutor without the previous knowledge, advice, and consent of the superintendent;

7. that it should at all times allow the superintendent audience.

In reference to the bookkeepers and deacons—they ought to assist the pastors by giving them their fatherly support both in things spiritual and in things temporal. [51]

When Chemnitz received the assurance that all parties were willing to abide by these conditions, since they were in line with the Church Order (Bugenhagen's 1528 Order as revised in 1563), he no longer had any reason to withhold his acceptance, and on Oct. 15, 1567, he was inducted into his new office as superintendent. The separation from Moerlin grieved him, but the faithful confession of God's will in word and deed established priorities for Chemnitz, so he bade Moerlin (who would live less than another four years) a fond and a sad farewell the following December. [52] Meanwhile, since the council wished to see its new superintendent clothed with the honor of a doctorate, it granted him a leave of absence and the municipality assumed the costs of his doctoral promotion, which he obtained at the age of 45 from the University of Rostock under Drs. Simon Pauli and David Chytraeus on June 30, 1568. He held a disputation "Concerning the Benefits of the Son of God, Our Lord and Redeemer, Jesus Christ" [53] and received the high approbation of the faculty. Bearing now, like the first Martin, the doctoral obligation to be a teacher of the Holy Scriptures, he returned to Brunswick to bring forth the mature fruit of his development. [54]

The Man—As Superintendent

About a month after his return to Brunswick the now "doctored" superintendent received an invitation from the new ruler of Brunswick-Wolfenbuettel, Duke Julius, to direct the establishment of the Reformation in his land. He had just come to power, his father, Duke Henry the Younger, having died in June of 1568. Henry died in the Evangelical faith although he had spent his entire reign combating it. He had attempted to force the old faith back upon the city of Brunswick but had been prevented from doing so by John Frederick of electoral Saxony and Philip of Hesse in 1545. However, after their defeat at Muehlberg in 1547 he returned to power, yet he had been sobered enough that after 1553 he granted the city the free exercise of the Evangelical faith, though he himself remained loyal to the pope until days before his death. His son Julius, who had been raised in the Evangelical faith under the influence of his mother, a princess from Wuerttemberg, had long felt the persecuting hand of his father, and to escape the same had sought refuge at the court of Duke Christoph of Wuerttemberg. Here also he had become acquainted with that duke's prominent theologians, especially Jakob Andreae. And it was to him that the duke turned when Chemnitz asked for a co-worker in the task of reforming the duke's territory. So it happened that Andreae and Chemnitz found themselves thrown together to do their Lord's (lord's) work in Brunswick-Wolfenbuettel in the late summer of 1568.[55]

Chemnitz arrived in Wolfenbuettel two weeks earlier than did Andreae, and he immediately set to work preparing a doctrinal statement composed of theses and antitheses to accompany the *corpus doctrinae* as authoritative interpretation thereof. When Andreae arrived, Chemnitz submitted his work to him for approval and rejoiced when this was readily given. They then also quickly agreed on a provisional church order, and thus armed initiated their visitation of the churches, monasteries, and schools. As they had expected, they found conditions appalling. Their remedy was drastic—every pastor or teacher who was either unwilling to subscribe the Augsburg Confession or who was simply incompetent in office was required to resign. This resulted in a terrible shortage of pastors and teachers, to overcome which Andreae attempted to enlist help back in Wuerttemberg. However, the response was minimal, and he used humor to cover his disappointment when he wrote Chemnitz that his compatriots were reluctant to be called "aus dem Wein- in ein Bierland."[56]

Chemnitz proceeded to put the finishing touches on the new church order which would regulate parish life in Brunswick-Wolfenbuettel, and by Jan. 1, 1569, Duke Julius could date his preface to it and write:

> Accordingly in the churches and schools of this territory it is henceforth allowable to teach nothing else than what is in keeping and accordance with the herein documented *corpus doctrinae*. What is taught must have a good, clear, convincing basis in it, not only as pertains to substance but also as pertains to the very vocabulary. But

whatever is inconsistent with or opposed and contradictory to it, shall not be tolerated, but shall be rather avoided and rejected. [57]

Thus in 1569 the theologian, Chemnitz, and the enlightened Christian prince, Duke Julius, were yoked together as representatives of a dual approach to church order which combined into the strong confessional position which Andreae had yet to master—concordia by exclusion and when necessary by expulsion. [58]

A very important source of Chemnitz' influence on the developing confessional consciousness of Lutheran Christians, both clerical and lay, was the publication (1569) of his so-called *Enchiridion,* a commentary on his contributions to the *Corpus doctrinae Julium* and intended to be used in the preparation of the clergy for examinations conducted by the superintendent twice each year and for the examination of candidates for ordination. It was originally written in German so that its contents could also become familiar to the educated laity, who then could assist in holding the pastors to account. At the urging of Nikolaus Selnecker the book was not only printed but Duke Julius required that every pastor obtain a copy of it. It was this book by Chemnitz which as much as anything made possible the rapid growth of a strong confessional commitment in the church of Brunswick-Wolfenbuettel. [59]

Hand in hand with the reform of church structures goes the reform of the educational system. Julius took an important step in this direction when he made provisions for the establishment of an academy at Gandersheim in 1571. This was then moved to Helmstedt, 25 miles east of Brunswick, in 1574, and two years later it was raised to the level of a university. The charter was written in part by Chytraeus and Chemnitz, and the latter preached the dedicatory sermon. [60] It was the purpose of this educational institution not only to serve the needs of the state by the cultivation of the various sciences but it was also and particularly to serve as a support for the young territorial church and thus to round out and firmly establish the work of reformation. Accordingly the church-related character of the university had to correspond to the Lutheran character of the church order. Teachers in all the faculties were tested for their acquaintance and agreement with the same by a commission of which Chemnitz was an indispensable member. No one received an appointment to the university without his approval. This close cooperation between the university and the church administration ended in 1578 as a result of the controversy concerning the tonsure of the sons of Duke

Julius.[61] Such an arrangement raises, of course, interesting questions on the relation of education to church and state and on the nature of academic freedom and the freedom of conscience itself. This latter question, insofar as it applies to Chemnitz, can be considered in the context of a discussion of Chemnitz' immediate involvement with the formulation and implementation of the Formula of Concord.

The Man—As Concordist

The drive to formulate a confession which would establish peace among all the contending parties within Lutheranism originated, as we have already seen,[62] not with Chemnitz but with Andreae. Chemnitz was certainly also interested in establishing confessional unity among Lutherans, but he approached this task from a different point of departure. As one scholar has put it, "Chemnitz strebte einen Kirchenbund, Andreae eine Bundeskirche an," that is to say, Chemnitz' goal was a "league of churches" brought together through a process whereby the unit churches gradually grew into a league united by mutually accepted confessions, whereas Andreae's goal was a "state church" established more or less "on the spot" as the unit churches recognized as their own a confession which had been drawn up independently of them and which they now had only to subscribe in order to make public their consent.[63] Therefore when Andreae arrived in Wolfenbuettel with a "finished" confession in his briefcase and looked for subscribers among the churches and pastors of northern Germany, Chemnitz reacted very coolly, going so far as to write a pastor in reference to Andreae's confession: "Supposedly a new apostle has arisen who desires to prescribe new articles of faith."[64] To his friend Moerlin Chemnitz wrote in the spring of 1570: "There is an attempt being made to put down the controversies with the fist, i. e., by force. They want to quarter the Flacians, and then do the same to their adherents. Thereupon we are to enjoy peace and tranquillity. This is proclaimed not only in threatening and harsh words, but I fear something is being attempted here which our dear God will condemn."[65]

At the authorization of the Brunswick ministerium Chemnitz composed what was to serve as a counterpart to Andreae's "Five Articles," and it was signed by the ministerium on May 17, 1570. In addition to the articles treated by Andreae, Chemnitz included an article on predestination and on the question of the doctrinal norm. In reference to the latter he wrote that Melanchthon's writings were to be interpreted not contrary to but in accordance with Luther's and that the writings of both were to be subjected to the Confessions. He insisted that true unity presupposed pure doctrine, which in turn demanded the isolation and condemnation of specific false teachings, even though, for the sake of fairness, these ought not be absolutely associated with specific persons. [66]

Chemnitz was soon involved in open opposition to the "New Wittenbergers" as distinguished from the "Old Wittenbergers." The former had published a catechism in 1571 to which Chemnitz took outspoken exception. Particularly galling to him was the use this catechism made of Acts 3:21 to establish the notion that Christ's body was restricted to a particular location in heaven. Even though most modern translators agree with the translation of this passage as given in the Wittenberg Catechism, Chemnitz was nevertheless correct in refusing to let this translation determine what God might and might not give in the Sacrament. [67] But the "New Wittenbergers" were determined to undermine the credibility of their opponent, whose reputation as an orthodox, evangelical, Biblical Lutheran scholar continued to grow, all the more so since the appearance in 1570 of the first edition of his monumental *De duabus naturis in Christo.* [68] In defending himself, now, against the charges of the Wittenbergers, Chemnitz looked for support from confessional Lutherans everywhere and thus, perhaps, became more amenable to the suggestion of Andreae that they arrive at a formula which would unite all loyal Lutherans. [69]

Additional encouragement was given Chemnitz to this end by the fact that Duke Julius and other concerned princes were giving their explicit support to Andreae's proposals and also by the fact that Elector August of Saxony was getting wise to the tactics of the Crypto-Calvinists in his territory and soon would send them scurrying. [70] When, therefore, a copy of Andreae's *Six Christian Sermons* was placed in Chemnitz' hands (spring of 1573), he was in a receptive mood, and the new tone of "concordia by exclusion" as reflected in the *Sermons* was music to his ears. He actually heard Andreae saying "that not a new confession was to be established but only a unanimous consensus, stated in theses and antitheses, regarding those articles which being contested; this consensus in turn was to be unanimously subscribed by the churches and theologians of Swabia and Lower Saxony and thus published." [71] This was almost beyond Chemnitz' rosiest dreams.

The story of how these dreams became a reality through the painful process eventuating in the publication of the Formula of Concord has already been told.[72] There remains in this place only the need to add a few details such as will help us to understand this document from the perspective of that formulator who most of all is responsible for its "orthodox" theological content and tone.

As the suggestions for the improvement of the "Torgau Book" were being considered by Chemnitz and the others at Bergen Abbey in 1577, he wrote in a letter to Duke William at Celle: "Finally there must be a limit set to this theological one-upmanship, if we don't in the end wish to lose the entire substance."[73] It was becoming clear to Chemnitz that there was a limit to the success one could expect in establishing a unanimous confession through a process of "participatory democracy." There came a time when he felt responsible leadership simply had to call for obedience. Thus we find evidence that not only had Chemnitz succeeded in modifying Andreae's notions of how to achieve unity, but that the reverse was also probably true.[74]

Whether or not Chemnitz, like Andreae, felt himself obligated to pamper the sensitivities of the secular rulers in order to guarantee their support for his concordistic activity, or whatever, is dramatically illustrated by the events surrounding the abrupt dismissal of Chemnitz from the consistory by Duke Julius in December of 1578. Earlier that year the duke still placed explicit confidence in Chemnitz as his theological adviser, for he both solicited and followed the latter's advice in reference to the request coming from Queen Elizabeth of England that he participate in a league of all Evangelical princes for the purpose of defending Protestantism against the renewed power of the Roman Church. Chemnitz gave him an arsenal of theological answers as to why this should not be done and was sure that Julius himself was aware of the political reasons for not doing so.[75] But the duke's confidence in Chemnitz (a confidence which had been expressed continuously over a 10-year period) collapsed when Chemnitz approached him like a Nathan encountering a David and announced: "Thou art the man!"

Of what was Julius guilty?—He had violated the Formula of Concord's stand on adiaphora by permitting his 14-year-old Lutheran son, the later Duke Henry Julius (1564—1613), to receive the tonsure (along with two of his brothers) at the hands of the Roman Catholic Abbot of Huyseburg and having him formally introduced into his see with the traditional Roman Catholic rite and ceremonial.[76] To Chemnitz and most of his Evangelical brethren it appeared to be a clear case of aiding and abetting the enemy through confessional negligence.[77] To

Julius it was merely a matter of taking advantage of a good business deal, for he had no intention of joining or encouraging the Roman Church as such. And to Andreae it was an occasion which called for the utmost in tact in the hope both that Julius might more easily be moved to repentance once the spotlight was off him and that meanwhile his support for the Formula of Concord might not be lost. [78]

As matters turned out the duke ultimately receded from his outright rejection of Chemnitz, but their old intimacy was never restored, even though at a formal level the duke arranged to be represented at the wedding of one of Chemnitz' daughters. Later he withdrew his subscription to the Book of Concord on a technicality. [79]

The relationship between Chemnitz and Andreae was also permanently affected as a result of their different attitudes in dealing with the case. This became evident when the two met at Bergen Abbey in February of 1580 to work through a final revision of the Preface to the Formula of Concord. [80] Chemnitz was unable to cover his wounded feelings at what appeared to him to have been a double cross on Andreae's part. The latter attempted to take the heat off himself by turning it back upon Chemnitz when Chemnitz suggested that certain "compromises" be made in the Preface. Chemnitz finally gave in to Andreae but did so only for the sake of bringing the work to a close. Thereafter each took to verbally accusing the other of treachery, [81] and the gossip circuit was loaded with the cross currents of partisan supporters, overwhelmingly pro-Chemnitz. Elector August helped establish at least a visible cessation of hostilities by requesting both of them to carry through a visitation at the University of Jena, at the conclusion of which they were "reconciled." [82]

The completion of the Formula of Concord, however, did not initiate a period of leisure during which the aging Chemnitz could have completed for publication a number of partially written manuscripts. Not until after his death did Polycarp Leyser publish Chemnitz' *Loci theologici* (1591), his *Harmonia evangelica* (1593), and his *Postilla* (1593). [83] While he could still summon his strength, Chemnitz was rather called upon to assist Selnecker and Kirchner with the writing and publication of the "Erfurt Apology of the Formula of Concord" (1582). [84] Much to his chagrin the representatives of Duke Julius from Helmstedt University, who met in secret session at Quedlinburg (50 miles southeast of Wolfenbuettel) with Chemnitz and other theologians representing Elector August, were unwilling to concede the "openness" of the Formula of Concord on the question of the ubiquity of Christ's glorified humanity. A key role in the refusal was played by Heshusius, who was nursing hurt feelings incurred when Chemnitz failed to support him in his controversy with Wigand and who also was probably reluctant to incur the duke's wrath and another exile (he already had experienced exile seven times). [85] Thus the university which Chemnitz had been so instrumental in getting off to an "orthodox" start [86] in the end accused its founding father of selling out to the "ubiquitists."

The experience of such lack of Christian love in the midst of conflicting claims to dogmatic orthodoxy seemed to contribute to the now steady decline in Chemnitz' health. He experienced depressions and frequently when visited by his friends would sob and weep uncontrollably, which his enemies hastily ascribed to pangs of conscience stemming from his involvement with the concordistic project. His robust health ebbed away over a seven-year period as a malarialike fever took its toll. Already by 1584 he was experiencing difficulty in walking, and when he noticed frequent lapses of memory and faltering speech he recommended to the city council that it accept his resignation. It in turn suggested that he take a leave of absence to recoup his strength, but after a few months he carried through his resolve and bade the ministerium farewell on Sept. 9, 1584. He expected 1585 to be his last year on earth, especially since the stars suggested to him that he would experience great difficulty during the month of March. However, nothing untoward occurred other than that he was forced to observe the passing of several friends and supporters. Easter of 1586 he celebrated in the circle of his family, his dutiful sons Martin, now aged 24, and Paul, aged 20, also being present. On the Thursday after Easter he was overcome with chills, and the following day two pastors came and brought him comfort from God's Word. He listened attentively and nodded affirmatively when he could no longer speak. Shortly before midnight on April 8, 1586, at the age of 64 years, of which 32 were spent in the holy ministry, this "second Martin," "bishop" of Brunswick and confessor, died. [87]

The Man—His Place in History

Since he was such a bold and outspoken confessor, any evaluation of Chemnitz will tend to reflect the evaluator's own confessional bias. But since Chemnitz was at the same time also "a gentleman and a scholar," the reaction to him, on the part of friends and foes alike, will usually call forth at least the attempt at exercising similar virtues. If forced to choose between confessionalists, more people would likely choose Chemnitz than Andreae. He appeared to have a certain humility, moderation, and quiet persistence which in the long run will probably always be more attractive to the majority of people than the traits attaching to the mercurial personality of an Andreae. But it is doubtful that the Formula of Concord could ever have come into being had it not been for the happy combination of gifts and talents which resulted when Chemnitz and Andreae found themselves ordained to work together in Wolfenbuettel in 1568.

If one were to draw Luther, Melanchthon, and Brenz into the comparison, perhaps one could say that Luther's gifts were divided between Andreae and Chemnitz, the former inheriting Luther's more adventurous, aggressive, crusading qualities and the latter his more domestic, settled, Renaissance virtues. And whereas it was Brenz who helped Andreae develop the crusader side of Luther, it was Melanchthon who aided Chemnitz in developing Luther's Renaissance characteristics. Andreae had more of the bumptious, experimental young Luther in him and Chemnitz more of the domesticated, balanced old Luther. And just as the old Luther ultimately to an extent tamed the young Luther, so in the Formula of Concord we have the product of an Andreae tamed by a Chemnitz.

One of Chemnitz' major contributions in the Lutheran consolidation process was his further development of the historical method in carrying on polemics.[88] His literary legacy gave to Lutheranism a historical awareness which it has neglected only at its peril. However, the fact that this historical interest was so exclusively used to serve a polemical and partisan cause is perhaps its own historically conditioned limitation. The method slowly had to be subjected to the more exacting criteria of a later age.

Perhaps an even more significant contribution made by Chemnitz to the developing image of Lutheranism was his persistent concern to preserve Luther's insight that "theology is more a total orientation than it is mere knowledge."[89] An important reason why one is able to find logical inconsistencies within Chemnitz' theology, when it is understood simply as a system, is the fact that his pastoral concern outweighs for him the need to have a logically neat and airtight system of doctrine. His Christology, for instance, explodes the framework he prepares for it in his twofold assertion that Jesus is without qualification true man and that, at the same time, there is an inner, indissoluble communion between His human nature and His divine nature. The tension between these two assertions is so great that it blows the logical constructs of the human mind. But Chemnitz far prefers this to robbing man's guilty conscience of the comfort given him by a Jesus who fully and completely identifies with man while He at the same time divinely overcomes all of man's sinfully induced limitations. Yet it is probably also true that Chemnitz does so more because he is an honest interpreter of the Scriptures and a faithful disciple of Luther than because he like Luther was existentially rescued from the yawning jaws of hell by the immediate experience of the evangelical right hand of God snatching him out of this hopeless peril.[90]

Of primary concern to Chemnitz, as it was to Luther, was that the certainty of salvation not be lost. Scholars, however, are still debating whether the two theologians defend the notion in the same way. Whereas some maintain that Luther tied certainty to the evangelical content of Scripture whereas Chemnitz tied certainty to Scripture's plenary inspiration, others argue that both Luther and Chemnitz were committed to the latter view. It would appear that the question is still in need of further discussion, with greater readiness on both sides to listen to the full range of evidence.[91]

On the question of the relationship between church and state Chemnitz seems to follow Luther more closely than does Andreae. As we have seen, Andreae sometimes had difficulty in distinguishing between his temporal lord and the Lord of lords.[92] In this respect Chemnitz was more careful—not in the sense that he avoided "politics" but in the sense that he meticulously distinguished between political and theological concerns without separating them. Like Andreae he appreciated the value and support of an Evangelical prince, but when he found it necessary to become involved with them he would pray beforehand: "Lead me not into temptation!"[93] He came closest to denying his own better principles when he followed his culture's commonly accepted practice of employing "expulsion" to effect "concord," thus using a power other than that of the Word to achieve a spiritual end. The fact that it was the temporal government which implemented the expulsion does not entirely remove the difficulty, since the government did so upon recommendation from the spiritual authorities, who made the recommendation ostensibly for spiritual reasons. Thus Chemnitz' understanding of religious liberty was altogether within the framework of his historical context, viz., German territorialism.

Chemnitz wanted to die as one whose confession was firmly

grounded "on the prophetic and apostolic Scriptures of the Old and New Testaments."[94] His favorite passage from Scripture pointed him to the living Center of the written word, and it became the basis for the sermon preached at his funeral by his coadjutor and friend, Johannes Zanger.—"I have been crucified with Christ; it is no longer I who live, but Christ who lives in me; and the life I now live in the flesh I live by faith in the Son of God, who loved me and gave Himself for me"[95] (Gal. 2:20). Was it also "in the stars" that Chemnitz should receive burial on "Quasimodogeniti" Sunday in the echo of the antiphon: "As newborn babes, Alleluia! Desire the sincere milk of the Word. Alleluia!"?

DAVID CHYTRAEUS
—ALTER PHILIPPUS?

Historical memory of the Reformation period would doubtless assign the years 1530 and 1531 to Philip Melanchthon, who at that time gave to the Lutheran Church its foundational theological statements, the Augsburg Confession and its Apology. A son born into a Lutheran parsonage during these years of Melanchthon's most significant theological achievements should somehow have been marked by the spirit of this great Biblical humanist and theologian, and precisely such was the case with David Chytraeus. David's father, Matthew Kochhafe,[1] was Lutheran pastor for the village of Ingelfingen (near Schwaebisch-Hall and about 50 miles to the east of Melanchthon's birthplace at Bretten). Here David was born on Feb. 26, 1531 (just 10 days after his famous mentor's 34th birthday). Perhaps it was in reaction to the somewhat traumatic experiences surrounding his birth that David grew up basically shy, lacking self-confidence, and with a great penchant for avoiding violence and maintaining peace. At any rate the story is told that his father refused to reinstate the Mass in 1530 in spite of rumors that Charles V would force Evangelicals to do so with the sword. On one occasion he preached against this order in the presence of an imperial official who became so angered over Kochhafe's insubordination that he drew his sword and stormed the pulpit. God protected Matthew, but his wife was so shocked by what she witnessed that she could neither cry nor speak for an hour. Immediately thereafter she gave birth to David.[2]

David, however, was a healthy baby and, as his parents were soon to discover, precocious to boot—a veritable second Philip Melanchthon. What did this childhood similitude to "Philip" mean for David, one of the future formulators of the Formula of Concord? To what extent would the child be father of the man?

The Child

By the time he was seven Chytraeus was receiving private instruction from pastors in the vicinity of Menzingen, where his father was now serving two knights, the brothers Erasmus and Peter, as pastor. It was soon evident, however, that Chytraeus was ripe for the university, so at the tender age of eight or nine he matriculated at the University of Tuebingen, where within a couple of years he must have met a student later to become a colleague and "thorn," Jakob Andreae.[3] Life at the *Stift* (a live-in seminary) was closely regulated and thus suited the highly disciplined Chytraeus fine. There is no record that his "wine privileges" were ever revoked for tardiness or that he ever did *Carcerstrafe* (solitary confinement) for dancing or drunkenness.[4]

Though he spent some time studying law, philology, and philosophy, he soon settled down to theology and had as teachers men like Joachim Camerarius (1500—74), the biographer of Melanchthon and his assistant in preparing the Apology of the Augsburg Confession; Erhard Schnepf (1495—1558), who was so influential in shaping the thinking of Jakob Andreae;[5] and Deacon Jakob Heerbrand (1521—1600), the author of a *Compend of Theology* which was so widely used that it was even translated into Greek.[6] Camerarius must have provided the young Chytraeus with a yearning to study under Melanchthon himself, whereas Schnepf and Heerbrand acquainted him with basic Lutheranism. When only 14 years of age Chytraeus was honored with the master's degree and happily proceeded to Wittenberg to study with the "giants" (1544).

Armed with letters of recommendation, one from Brenz directed to Luther and another from Georg Schwarzerdt addressed to his brother, Philip Melanchthon, Chytraeus was soon invited to board with the Melanchthon family, and he became one of Philip's favorite pupils, spending more than five years in his home.[7] It was Melanchthon who encouraged Chytraeus to develop his encyclopedic interests while reminding him of Pliny's advice not to read much superficially but much thoroughly. This thoroughness he was also to apply to his reading of the Bible and the *Loci* and to his prayer life.

Chytraeus considered it his special fortune that he was still able to sit at Luther's feet. He heard Luther lecture on the last 11 chapters of Genesis[8] and listened to him preach the Gospel from the pulpit of the City Church. A sermon Luther preached on Christmas 1545 etched itself on his memory. Luther was making reference to the traditional Old Testament lesson on that day and spent almost an hour expounding the words: "For to US a child is born, to US a son is given" (Is. 9:6). Finally he concluded with the words: "Blessed and truly Christian is the theologian who with certainty believes that this child is born FOR US, that he is OUR righteousness, OUR forgiveness of sins."[9] Obviously Chytraeus had been touched by the evangelical character of Luther's preaching.

As was the case with Chemnitz (who was also in Wittenberg at this time), so Chytraeus too was forced to break off his studies at Wittenberg as a result of the disturbances occasioned by the Smalcald War.[10] He spent a semester at Heidelberg (1546/47) and then one in Tuebingen (1547). In addition to hearing lectures on classical philology, Hebrew, and theology, he also with great interest heard Philip Imser lecture on astrology.[11] As soon as the University of Wittenberg was reopened (early 1548), Chytraeus returned and at Melanchthon's advice and with his support began to hold private lectures on rhetoric, astronomy, and the *Loci* of Melanchthon. He was a popular teacher, much appreciated by his students because of the clarity and perspicuity of his lectures and his friendly concern for the individual needs of these young scholars.[12]

Chytraeus enjoyed traveling and expanding his firsthand acquaintance with different places and different people. Thus it is not surprising that we find him in 1550 accompanying his colleague Johann Aurifaber to Rostock, where the latter had just accepted an appointment as professor and pastor. While there, Chytraeus favorably impressed certain faculty members who promised they would strongly recommend him to the dukes for a professorial appointment. Meanwhile he further indulged his travel urge by visiting Italy and Switzerland, everywhere playing the keen observer and establishing contacts with learned and interesting people wherever he could. And when he returned to Wittenberg early in 1551 he discovered that he was about to leave both his teens and his carefree student days behind.

The Father

The offer from the Dukes of Mecklenburg, Heinrich and Johann Albrecht, to accept a professorship at the University of Rostock did not exactly catch Chytraeus by surprise. He held his first lecture on April 21, 1551, and since he was a bare 20 years of age he was for the first entrusted with lectures in philosophy (history) rather than theology.[13] One had to earn his spurs in philosophy before presuming to lecture on the queen of sciences. His theological interests, however, were betrayed even when he was lecturing on Herodotus, for he had a special attraction for commenting on the Second Book. It just happened to contain a description of Egypt, and Chytraeus enjoyed demonstrating how here and there the development of the subject by Herodotus agreed with that of the Holy Scriptures.[14] A more directly theological lecture was permitted Chytraeus in the academy, where students with deficiencies could have them removed before entering the university. Here Chytraeus delivered a commentary on the catechisms of Melanchthon. This was eventually published (*Catechesis,* 1554) and became a popular dogmatics for nonprofessional use that was published in edition after edition for a century.

When Chytraeus arrived at the university, it had not yet completed its own reorganization as necessitated by the introduction of the Reformation to Rostock particularly through the efforts of Joachim Slueter (ca. 1531). In carrying out this task Chytraeus was to play a leading role. But first providence would allow him an opportunity to secure his own position.

Beginning in 1553 Chytraeus' lectures at the university were more and more devoted to theology, although after 1575 history began again to predominate.[15] Now that he was publicly committed to the heavenly queen of sciences, perhaps he considered himself mature enough to commit himself to an earthly queen also. This he did by marrying Margaretha Smedes, the daughter of a prominent senator in Rostock. She bore him seven children, only two of whom (both daughters) reached adulthood. Margaretha herself died in 1571. About a year later Chytraeus married again, a Margaretha Pegel. Of this union two sons survived, Ulrich and David, neither of whom became prominent. Chytraeus is said to have ruled his house as a faithful husband and a loving father. Death was a persistent visitor at his home, and he himself was frequently and increasingly ill during the last 33 years of his life (1567—1600).[16] This undoubtedly goes far in explaining why the cross held such a central position in his theology, for he said:

> . . . neither the accumulated wisdom of all the earth and the skies, nor languages, church fathers, and daily reading of the Holy Scripture, nor immense learning and eloquence make a good theologian if the cross is not added, through which God purifies, cleanses, strengthens, and perfects the light of His true knowledge, of true faith in Christ, of true understanding of the divine promises, proper prayer, hope, humility, and all the virtues which He has first planted in the heart through the Word. Those are secure spirits rather than real men who live each day happily and joyfully, thinking that when they read the lament of an Ezekiel, the prayer of a Jonah, and other Psalms, they

are hearing only empty words and vain dreams; therefore they can neither understand these descriptions of a faith struggling under the heaviest of trials nor can they speak of them to others. Accordingly we should equip ourselves for the cross, which is just as necessary for those who wish to become good theologians as air and food are for the maintenance of the body. Since then the entire doctrine of the Gospel is a comfort for those who are bent and beaten with the feeling of the wrath of God and heavy trials, how should a person be able to understand the Gospel or teach it to others if he himself has not experienced the power of the Gospel in the midst of sorrows and trials?[17]

Thus it would seem that though Chytraeus had a firm grasp on Paul's (and Luther's) "theology of the cross" as expressed, for example, in Phil. 3:8-11, 17-21, and 2 Cor. 12:7-10, this theology is developed without adequate elaboration of Paul's "theology of signs and wonders" as recorded in Rom. 15:18-19; 1 Cor. 12:1-11; 2 Cor. 12:12. He recognizes that faith in the Gospel issues in an experience of the power of the Gospel, but that experience seems overly restricted to the virtue of patience in suffering without the other signs manifesting the lordship of Jesus and His victory over the enemy now. The great Biblical humanist seems to be having difficulty in his struggle to distinguish the "cross of Christ" from the "cross of the Stoics."

Chytraeus had intentions of completing a commentary on the entire Holy Scriptures. Within his lifetime two great collected editions of his exegetical works were published, a fact which is far from adequately explained by characterizing these works as being "glossatory, dogmatizing commentaries of slight importance."[18] His commentaries treated the first eight books of the Bible, selected Psalms, Micah, Nahum, Habakkuk, Zechariah, Malachi, Sirach, Matthew, John, Romans, and Revelation. An example of their practical and edifying character is furnished in his *De sacrificiis,* published as a prolegomenon to his commentary on Leviticus.[19]

The year 1555 marked the publication of Chytraeus' *Regulae vitae,* which has merited attention as the first ethics textbook in the Lutheran Church. It reflects, however, the continued dependence of Chytraeus upon Melanchthon, since it is only a slight reworking of Melanchthonian materials. The Decalog furnishes the outline, which then is filled in with comments and examples from classical antiquity and history to illustrate the various points.[20]

A strong impact on Chytraeus was that made by Tilemann

Heshusius (1527—88) during the short period when they were colleagues at Rostock (1556—57). Chytraeus was particularly impressed when he observed how confident Heshusius was of the correctness of his theological position, whereas Chytraeus himself was still seeking such conviction in the midst of the raging theological confusion of the times. [21] In general, Chytraeus had a deep appreciation for his colleagues, even in their differences. He always felt they had something to teach him, something he could profitably learn. With such an attitude it is no wonder that they elected him to the rectorate of the university six times, an honor he jokingly said made him the institution's "general handyman." [22] His popularity in academic circles was not restricted to Rostock, for by 1557 he had already received calls to five different universities, and before his last call in 1581 he would receive 10 more such offers. The fact that he remained in Rostock reflects the ability of his dukes, now Johann Albrecht and Ulrich, and his colleagues to exercise their considerable persuasive powers upon a congenitally gentle, peace-loving soul. [23]

Chytraeus loved the stimulation and opportunities for learning which extensive travel afforded, so it is not surprising that in 1557 while on a trip to visit his relatives in southern Germany he took the time to play the tourist in Friesland, Holland, Brabant, and Flanders. The humanist in him must have rejoiced as it thus picked up the trail of the vaunted Erasmus. But within a month he was unhappily to experience that which pained every true humanist, the "madness of the theologians." [24] The occasion was his participation in the infamous Colloquy at Worms, which was to be followed a year later (1558) by his sharp critique of the Melanchthon-inspired Frankfurt Recess. [25] A strain in the relationship between Chytraeus and Melanchthon began to appear.

In Chytraeus' record book duplicity earned bad grades. He abhorred it in doctrinal formulations and rejected it in personal relationships. However, in attempting to maintain this high moral standard he fell into another kind of duplicity, that of the "man for all seasons," Sir Thomas More. More lived his conscience, and where he couldn't he chose silence. He never really committed himself verbally, until it was too late, on the question of Henry's jurisdiction over the church. Thus, though he died for the right of private judgment, he acquiesced in the duplicity of silence. [26] And so it would seem that since Chytraeus preferred silence to a forthright judgment on Melanchthon's orthodoxy, he too chose to bear this guilt as the lesser of several evils. [27] Nevertheless, inwardly he had come to a fork in the road in his relationship to Melanchthon, and as a result he could eventually "in his own way" belong to the "Center-Party," from whose midst there arose the formulators of the Formula of Concord. [28]

The year 1561 found Chytraeus emerging more and more as the chief spokesman for the theological faculty at Rostock. His respected mentor Melanchthon had died (April 19, 1560), and perhaps his passing gave Chytraeus more courage to speak his own mind. He himself was honored with a theological doctor's degree (April 29, 1561) and already before that had been chosen to accompany Duke Ulrich to the Convention of Princes at Naumburg (Jan. 21—Feb. 8, 1561). [29] When Duke Johann Albrecht asked his theologians for an evaluation of the Naumburg Recess, it was Chytraeus who composed the same on behalf of his colleagues and therein offered a scathing denunciation of Crypto-Calvinism. [30] And if further evidence is needed to demonstrate the increasing commitment on the part of Chytraeus to an unequivocal Lutheran position, one need only contemplate the following statement of his guiding principle:

> It is God's immutable will and command that all novice preachers and ministers of Christ not only diligently preach the true doctrine as with one mind, correctly and unadulterated, but also that they should refute and reject false and erring doctrines and warn their listeners regarding those who are false teachers and seducers and point the finger at and name by name the wolf who is sneaking about in their midst in sheep's clothing, in order that the lambs might be able to protect themselves from him and make their escape. It is impossible that simple souls defend themselves against false teachers who employ such beautiful, sweet talk, unless one designates them by name. Since now the errors of the Anabaptists, the Sacramentarians, the Schwenkfeldians, Osiandrians, Stancarians, and others contradict the Word of God, it is accordingly proper that faithful preachers not be dumb dogs but should joyfully and confidently rebuke by name false teachers and their doctrine, refute and condemn such doctrine, and point the finger at and explicitly name the wolf who is sneaking into their midst dressed in sheep's clothing. [31]

In the years immediately following Naumburg, Chytraeus was absorbed in efforts to reorganize the University of Rostock. A major breakthrough occurred when in 1563 he was instrumental in effecting an agreement between the ruling house and the city council relative to combined patronage of the university. As rector he then proceeded in the following year to establish new university statutes, those affecting the theological faculty being of special concern to him. The statutes called for doctrinal consensus based on the prophetic and apostolic Scriptures interpreted in keeping with the ecumenical creeds, the Augsburg Confession, the Smalcald Articles, and Luther's writings in general. The territorial consistory which was established in 1571, to the chairmanship of which Chytraeus was immediately elected, also reflected this strongly Lutheran orientation.[32]

The year 1566 found Chytraeus accompanying Duke Ulrich to the Diet of Augsburg, an occasion which deeply saddened him as he witnessed the Crypto-Calvinism of the new Wittenbergians. To his friend Marbach he wrote: "The Sacramentarians have erected the citadel for their false doctrine in the very heart of Germany, and already one hears the public applause at the courts and from the intellectuals at the schools."[33] However, his firm and sober Lutheranism coupled with his peace-loving disposition and his ecclesiastical vision did not go unnoticed. In 1567 Duke John William (Jena) commissioned him to write in the name of the Rostock faculty an evaluation of "The Weimar Book of Confutation."[34] One had come to expect from Chytraeus a judgment that was Scriptural, Lutheran, and fair-minded. His reputation was established, and the church on a broader scale now sought the services of this mature, learned, and Christian man.

The Man—As Reformer in Austria

The now 38-year-old Chytraeus was the man whom Emperor Maximilian II singled out to organize an Evangelical church in Austria. Actually he was the emperor's third choice, but one which the emperor never regretted.[35] It is altogether possible that Chytraeus came to the attention of the emperor while both attended the Diet of Augsburg in 1566, the diet at which Maximilian disappointed the Protestants by his refusal to grant them universal freedom of religion, although he soon thereafter afforded Evangelicals in the archduchy of Austria a series of concessions. Protestants had long hoped that Maximilian would allow his sympathy for their theological concerns to shape his political decisions in reference to them, but in this hope they gradually discovered themselves to have been excessively sanguine. Nevertheless, those Evangelicals who could still think in terms of a possible reunion of Protestantism with Rome continued to find in Maximilian II a reasonable conversation partner. And in spite of (or because of?) his pronounced Lutheran profile, such an Evangelical was Chytraeus.[36]

The Twelve Days of Christmas 1568 did not find Chytraeus enjoying the sound of Christmas carols as he sat with his family around the parsonage fireplace. Instead, he was making the cold journey to Krems (ca. 40 miles northwest of Vienna), where he arrived on Jan. 10, 1569. However, on the way he was able to share a little Christmas cheer with Chemnitz and Andreae in Wolfenbuettel, and it is not difficult to imagine what the three talked about. It was not the weather![37]

Evangelicals in Austria at this time were for the most part like sheep without a shepherd. Those serving as shepherds frequently appeared to be little more than "hirelings," i. e., pastors from abroad who had been dismissed from office at home because of their sectarian behavior and who now provided Austrian Evangelicals with a cheap source of ready-to-go clergy. The results for the flock in Austria were predictable—sheer chaos. It was to face and remedy this intolerable situation that Maximilian called Chytraeus, who was to prepare a church order in harmony with the Augsburg Confession, using the oldest Evangelical orders as models, viz., those of Saxony and Brandenburg-Nuernberg.[38] These basically conservative/ecumenical documents of the Lutheran Reformation were in keeping with the expectations of Maximilian and his trusted adviser Lazarus von Schwendi, both of whom greatly desired the reunification of the churches, and this to be effected under the leadership not of the pope, nor of the theologians and their individual princes, but of the emperor. Melanchthon too had once shared this ideal, and now it served as the goal toward which his peace-loving former student Chytraeus set out to work, perhaps with the vision that if it could be realized in Austria, why not in the remainder of the empire?[39]

Four representatives of the Evangelical estates authorized Chytraeus to draw up on their behalf a number of separate documents for presentation to the emperor: a church agenda, an order for the consistory, a commentary on the individual articles of the Augsburg Confession (later referred to as the *Doctrinale*), and a concise epitome of the doctrinal position *(Examen ordinandorum)*. Chytraeus tackled the task immediately and within two months, with the assistance of Christoph Reiter, a local friend who knew the problems firsthand, he had completed a draft of the agenda, which he immediately sent to the emperor for approval. This the latter granted, but realizing that there was more to come, he reminded Chytraeus: "My orders were to prepare an agenda, not a dogmatics text."[40] As anxious as Chytraeus was to see a union effected, he apparently had no intention of buying it by a cheap avoidance of the doctrinal issues.

By the end of March 1569 Chytraeus arrived in Vienna with finished products in hand and prepared to negotiate with the emperor and the estates regarding their acceptance. The discussions focused particularly on two points: the ceremonials and the recognition of episcopal jurisdiction. In reference to the first point the emperor had wished ceremonial as close to the traditional as possible. But the estates objected to ceremonial such as the wearing of Eucharistic vestments, the lighting of candles, and particularly the elevation of the host at the celebration of the Sacrament. Since Chytraeus had acceded to the wishes of the estates, the emperor said to him: "Your industry and your faithfulness in preparing the 'Church Agenda' pleases me. I notice, however, that frequently you were more concerned with pleasing the estates than with expressing your own opinion."[41]

In reference to the jurisdiction of bishops Chytraeus was happy to meet the emperor's concerns, namely, that the Evangelical preachers be ordained by the bishops according to a given formula, yet with due consideration to avoid sinful obligations. If bishops did not persecute or obstruct the Gospel, their jurisdiction was to be recognized. The estates were permitted to have one of their own pious, learned, and moderate preachers examine candidates for the ministry and to award them a certificate of approval, but they were not permitted to perform the rite of ordination itself.[42]

Chytraeus returned to Rostock in time to begin his lectures at the opening of the winter semester (Oct. 18, 1569). The emperor did not neglect to send glowing reports of the professor's accomplishments both to the dukes and to the university administration, but the glow of success faded very quickly for Chytraeus. He experienced deep chagrin that the agenda was not published until 1571 and that when it did finally appear it did so with unauthorized changes apparently made by the above-mentioned Reiter. In Chytraeus' mind they were changes for the worse, and he hated to see his name associated with the mangled remains of his agenda. A further source of irritation was that the *Doctrinale,* which for him had become a labor of love, was not even submitted for publication. As a result the chaotic conditions of the Evangelical Church in Austria were only compounded. After weeks of swallowing his gorge he finally wrote a public disavowal of responsibility for the whole mess.[43] The experience definitely soured him on the entire game of ecclesiastical politics, and it certainly affected the manner in which he would later respond to Andreae's concordistic proposals.

Though Chytraeus had been given reason to shake the dust of Austria off his feet, his heart bled for the victims of ecclesiastical intrigue there, and when finally in 1573 the estates of Styria (a duchy in southeast Austria) pleaded with him to come and assist them with ecclesiastical reform and with the establishment of an Evangelical *Gymnasium* to counter the effect of a newly erected Jesuit school near the royal palace grounds, he completely overcame his chagrin and with the permission of his dukes set out in a southerly direction in September of that year. After a series of delays he finally arrived in Graz (90 miles south of Vienna) in January of 1574. By the end of May Chytraeus could speak at the dedication of the new *Gymnasium* and also submit his proposed church order, one which frequently followed the stripped-down liturgical practices of the "Wuerttemberg Agenda" (1559) rather than the more eclectically traditional practices of the order for Austria (1571). The mood among the Evangelicals in Styria—and Chytraeus was swift to adapt to it—was strongly anti-Counter-Reformation. Undoubtedly his own recent experience in ecumenical churchmanship in Austria and the publication of Chemnitz' *Examen*[44] served to heighten his circumspection in questions relating to church union.

On his return to Rostock Chytraeus arranged to meet with Christoph Reiter and other of the Austrian theologians at Stein/Krems to discuss once more how some semblance of peace and unity might be achieved among the Austrian Evangelicals. He concentrated on two points of particular irritation: the Flacian doctrine of original sin and episcopal ordination. As to the first point he insisted that original sin was not to be conceived of as belonging to the substance or essence of man; nevertheless it did represent a "deep, dreadful corruption and ruination of our entire human nature." As for episcopal ordination he clearly placed it in the category of adiaphora when he wrote:

> For the public testimony of the presbytery, namely, that a given preacher has been called and examined, that he is qualified for the holy office of the ministry, that he has been authorized to preach and to administer the sacraments in the said churches, this together with the prayer that God would bless his calling and office, is what is properly meant by Christian ordination, even though in certain places, where one cannot obtain it, the external ceremonies together with the laying on of hands in a recognized church is not added.[45]

A final matter of grave concern to Chytraeus as he shared his thoughts with the Austrian theologians was the role of a synod in deciding doctrinal matters. His reservations are expressed as follows:

> The word "synod" is, to be sure, a beautiful one, and Christian synods ought to be held to deal with controversial matters, as did the apostles and later the pious emperors Constantine, Theodosius, and others. However, great dissension often arose out of synods, so much so that the learned and pious Bishop Nazianzus writes that he intended to hold no synod lest it be followed by still greater division and misery. Since, nevertheless, such church matters as are of general concern, especially those dealing with doctrinal questions, ought to be taken under consideration by informed, pious, and learned members of the church and thus finally approved, we propose the following plan: First, after our gracious lords together with their theologians have made a thorough study of the situation, they ought to arrange a meeting of three or four preachers within each circuit, choosing such as are known to be reasonable, peace-loving, modest, chaste, and learned men. The issues ought to be discussed with them privately and harmoniously settled. Thereupon one could inquire of them as to the leanings of their neighboring pastors in both doctrine and practice and decide whether a general synod of all or of the majority of Evangelical preachers ought to be convened.... However, it would be particularly valuable and highly desirable if the doctrinal position were to be confirmed and accepted by a harmonious consensus of the synod. But since it is impossible to convene a general synod for a long enough time to read through the entire doctrinal position carefully and with due deliberation and since there are many contentious, arrogant, obstinate, and presumptuous colleagues who are satisfied with nothing other than that which is shaped according to their own opinions, one of whom will readily contest this and the other that, we accordingly still think as we did three years ago in reference to the agenda that in view of such differences and disunity among the populace and their preachers the doctrinal statement ought not be made binding on one and all but should to begin with be obligatory only for those who voluntarily commit themselves to it and thereupon for all those about to be ordained or those who come to this country from the outside. Also we propose, therefore, that at this time such matters not be deliberated in a synod and that a general synod be altogether postponed.[46]

Having shared this advice with his Austrian friends, Chytraeus did not wait around to measure the effect but hastened his return to Rostock.

He perhaps suspected that he had been wasting his time and hoped that back in Rostock his above-outlined plan for achieving doctrinal consensus could be more realistically implemented, for Andreae and Chemnitz were already engaged in an attempt to formulate a doctrinal consensus and Chytraeus was understandably being drawn into the project.

The Man—As Concordist

At the end of 1569, after Chytraeus had returned to Rostock from his first trip to Austria, he received a visit from Andreae, whom he had consulted in Wolfenbuettel just a year before.[47] Andreae was interested in discussing with him his plans for achieving a *concordia* in the Evangelical camp, to which end he had already forwarded a copy of his "Five Articles" to Dukes Johann Albrecht and Ulrich for dissemination and discussion among their theologians.[48] But as far as Chytraeus was concerned, to have been in Austria was to have been forewarned. Although he was highly desirous of seeing a union of the contending parties effected, he was equally suspicious of achieving this by means of a privately authored document simply submitted to the churches for ratification. Against this presumption Chytraeus wrote in a document containing a confession of his own faculty relative to the subjects dealt with by Andreae in his "Articles":

> We hereby emphatically declare that we have composed this our confession for ourselves alone and in it have prescribed nothing for anyone else, far less desired to commend it or inflict it upon others as a *formula concordiae*. For we recognize ourselves to be far too inadequate and lacking in wisdom to be able to advise or do anything fruitful or beneficial relative to so many highly important matters and in a situation involving such bitter feelings not only between the theologians but also between high estates, feelings which have been stirred up in a variety of ways and as a result of their authors' own numerous calumnies. . . . If a Christian and salutary *concordia* is to be established, it must, as does the Augsburg Confession, not only set down the truth affirmatively but also reject falsehoods by name. May the almighty and eternal God graciously direct this highly important and doubtless well- and honestly-intentioned project, and insofar as we for our own persons are able to help in effecting a Christian, brotherly, and salutary union, we have, without boasting, conducted ourselves until now as godly, peace-loving, and faithful servants over against all alike.[49]

It is highly unlikely that Chytraeus intended these last words to be an encouragement to Andreae to try again, but Andreae chose to be a literalist and assumed that God was answering Chytraeus' prayer by prompting him to publish his *Six Sermons,* seasoned to order with the condemnation of false doctrines together with their authors.[50] Although the Lower Saxons were still not ready with their signatures, Joachim Westphal, the fiery anti-Calvinist and committed Lutheran superintendent of Hamburg, lent the weight of his support to Andreae's concordistic plans. In response Chytraeus proposed that a meeting of orthodox theologians be held, at which these plans should be thoroughly reviewed. Before Westphal could summon such a meeting, however, he died unexpectedly and his role was assumed by Chemnitz. The subsequent developments have already been related,[51] so here we have only to call special attention to the role of Chytraeus in it all.

That Chytraeus was highly qualified to serve on any committee commissioned to work out an authoritative interpretation of the Augsburg Confession goes almost without saying. He had been engaged in this task already while in Austria in 1569.[52] By 1576 he was able to publish his *Historia der Augsburgischen Confession,* which combines all the important documents pertaining to this basic Lutheran creed and ranks as the first effort at critical Reformation historiography.[53] During these years he also devoted himself to the study of the church fathers in order to determine their positions on the controversial questions of his own day. The more he discovered their disagreement on many points, the more he felt himself forced to turn steadfastly to the word of Scripture itself. Chemnitz' books also began to have a decisive influence on his theological convictions.[54] And when in 1574 Chemnitz sent him Andreae's "Swabian Concord" for evaluation, he preferred to rewrite two articles completely, viz., the second on Free Will and the seventh on the Lord's Supper. Chytraeus accurately sensed that if agreement could be reached on these two articles, the rest would come with relative ease. It is ironic, however, that precisely Chytraeus, who so detested privately authored confessions imposed on the church, could himself become so attached to his own contribution to the Formula of Concord that later, when it was severely abridged and edited, he could lament that "everything" he had written had been excised.[55] This is clearly an exaggeration and reflects typically an author's complaint about an editor, particularly an editor who had pique of his own.[56]

Chytraeus was among the 17 Lutheran theologians who met at

Torgau in 1576 to carry out the task of conflating the "Swabian-Saxon Concord" and the "Maulbronn Formula" into a single, precise, intelligible confession of faith.[57] The result was the "Torgau Book," and it was this early "unexpurgated" edition of the Formula of Concord to which Chytraeus really felt attached. After it had been replaced by the "Bergic Book,"[58] Chytraeus wrote to a friend:

If only the "Torgau Book," the form of the confession which had originally been subscribed and sent to the churches of the Augsburg Confession for approval, had also later been adhered to! However, the "Big Three," who were directing the project, had in my absence introduced at Bergen on the basis of the evaluations submitted by the churches, as they said, numerous expressions of Luther, particularly in reference to the bodily presence of Christ, which now alone are almost entirely responsible for the criticisms being hurled at the confession. I confess also that I, when finally after several months I was called in for consultation, subscribed the "Bergic Book"; however, not that Samaritan idol but only that doctrine which both before and after the Augsburg Confession has been commonly taught in our churches.[59]

It would seem from the above that Chytraeus understood his subscription to the "Bergic Book" in the form of a *quatenus* approval, i. e., insofar as it agreed with the Augsburg Confession. He also seemed to feel that when the invitation did finally come for him to participate at the second meeting at Bergen Abbey (i. e., in May of 1577 but not in March),[60] it was not his theological insights that were being solicited but only the church-political support which his participation would supposedly bring with it.[61]

So negatively did Chytraeus feel about the treatment which the "triumvirate" (Andreae, Chemnitz, and Selnecker) had accorded him by editing out in his absence so much of what he had written that he complained in a letter to Aegidius Hunnius (1550—1603):

Necessity compels me to avoid public controversies, particularly since I have learned in the meetings dealing with *The Book of Concord* that I of all people understand least how I am to conduct myself at the meetings. For Andreae, our "best of all rulers," sanctions nothing of all that I have said, done, or written, with the result that in the entire *Book of Concord* not a word stems from me. Accordingly I cannot be reckoned among its authors but only among its subscribers. Yet I have never retracted that which I once subscribed.[62]

Chytraeus obviously felt himself torn between his subscription of a document which he considered orthodox in its content and his negative feelings about the legalistic spirit he thought to have been prevailing at those final meetings as well as the manner in which he sensed the Formula was now being implemented. He agreed to the Formula insofar as it united the Evangelical churches. However, he did not consider it a means whereby those who believed otherwise should be dealt with, thus widening the communications gap. He saw the Formula as an aid in overcoming differences. Where it instead sharpened differences he considered it inadequate and hoped that a more convincing work would take its place, for he wrote:

> As far as I am concerned *The Book of Concord* clearly and firmly furnishes proofs and documentation from the Holy Scriptures and these will serve adequately until such a time as better and firmer arguments will be discovered by those who perhaps believe that here and there our theologians have strayed from the right path. [63]

The Rostock faculty stood firmly behind its spokesman, perhaps going so far as to register some of the occasions upon which "our theologians have strayed from the right path." For instance, in a letter to Andreae they indicate how they sense a discrepancy between the Formula and the Augsburg Confession together with its Apology in the cardinal doctrines dealing with justification and sanctification, conversion and good works, free will, and other articles. [64]

Perhaps we ought not be surprised that Chytraeus, who on the one hand was the "alter ego" of Melanchthon but who on the other hand had deeply felt the difference between Luther and Melanchthon and had been drawn decisively within the Lutheran camp, displays a certain *dissimulatio* in his stance over and against the Formula of Concord. [65] It is the strange dissimulation of one who having grasped the Gospel could follow Luther's pastoral advice, "Pecca fortiter." Chytraeus' Gospel-oriented sensibilities detected the ambivalence between "orthodoxy" and "evangelical conduct" as these wrestled for expression in the entire concordistic endeavor. And it threw the shadow of the cross over the rest of his life. In 1581 he published his *De morte et vita aeterna,* sometimes called the first Lutheran eschatology. It is said to be permeated with a Melanchthonian spirit, and because of it he was accused of going hand in hand with the Philippists and even of flirting with the Calvinists. [66] Actually it implicitly expressed Chytraeus' deepest Lutheran feelings that the Formula of Concord too belonged to a "theology of the cross" and ought not be blown up into a "theology of glory" by means of trumped-up claims.

The Man—Harvest Home

The stormy years of Chytraeus' activity in Austria and as concordist enabled a worm to enter the apple that was the harvest of his life. It was the worm of suspicion, and it was enough to raise the "Caveat emptor" sign over Chytraeus' contributions in the marketplace of ideas. For instance, his friends at the University of Helmstedt (which he had helped to found)[67] now saw no reason why his arguments in favor of their accepting the Formula of Concord should be convincing. They had only to witness Chystraeus' shift on the question of ubiquity to make them suspect that he was capable of playing chameleon theology. Chytraeus had, as a matter of fact, never been excited about this doctrine, but he was as a result of his concordistic involvement on the one hand honest enough to admit that the doctrine was not foreign to Luther and on the other hand evangelical enough to live with those for whom this belief was important although it was not so for him personally.[68]

The years following 1580 were undoubtedly years of *Anfechtung* for Chytraeus. He could easily have developed a humanist's scorn for the *rabies* as well as the *duritiam* of the theologians and thus have lost his own faith in the process. But a providential God understood how to chasten the brilliant student of Melanchthon with physical crosses and thus from under the cross to save his spirit in the day of the Lord Jesus. Chytraeus seemed to respond to this chastening of the Lord both by receiving it in faith, as his book *De morte et vita aeterna* attests, and by diverting his attention from the madness and stubbornness of the theologians to the more quiet pursuits of the professional historian. However, he soon discovered that the historian too has his hassles.

Of special importance among the published works of Chytraeus during this period are his *Metropolis* (first published 1582) and his *Sachsenchronik* (first published 1585). The former is essentially a catalog of bishops of the leading cities of northern Germany, prefaced by an extended introduction to the church history of northern Germany in the 16th century. The latter amounts to a history of northern Europe between 1500 and 1600, a sourcebook of information for historians of this period even today. Since Chytraeus was engaged in writing contemporary history, it was not long before one or the other of his contemporaries took issue with his interpretation of the facts. When this occurred it was particularly Duke Ulrich who applied pressure on Chytraeus to adjust the history so that his own political interests would not be damaged. This put a strain on Chytraeus' sense of academic integrity, but since he would be altogether unable to pursue his historical interests if he did not have the good will of those who frequently were the only people who could give him access to the sources, he was obliged to comply. [69] So not only as a theologian but also as a historian Chytraeus found it unavoidable that he live from the forgiveness of sins rather than from the spotlessness of his record.

Chytraeus' memory must certainly be associated with an entire genre of literature, viz., the so-called *Briefzeitungsliteratur*. By this term is meant that extensive correspondence of his which dealt particularly with the exchange of historically significant information for the purpose of making it available to the historian. To this end Chytraeus corresponded with government officials, pastors, university administrators, historians, bishops, generals, and even kings and princes. He received letters "postmarked" from places so diverse as Constantinople and Thessalonica, Sweden and Iceland, Antwerp and Amsterdam, and Russia. And to keep the flow of information moving he even maintained his own modest "pony express," which covered the long stretch between Livonia and Vienna. In this typically humanist activity Chytraeus even surpassed his mentor Melanchthon. [70] For the frequently bedridden scholar this ongoing involvement with matters other than his own aching and tormented body must have been a useful therapy.

During the last 20 years of his life Chytraeus excused himself for reasons of health from his frequently burdensome administrative tasks at the university. He devoted himself to his lectures, the publication of his books, and his correspondence. At last in his 69th year [71] the long-yearned-for redemption of the body came for Chytraeus, who was accustomed to say: "Here comes death, which heals and cleanses, which makes us all alike, and which brings victor and vanquished to the same goal." [72] Death came by way of a concurrence of various long-standing diseases taking advantage of a body suddenly greatly weakened by a severe catarrh. And it is perhaps a sign given by God to the Lutheran Church that He called His servant David home on June 25. It was the year 1600, the 70th anniversary of the presentation of Melanchthon's Augsburg Confession to Emperor Charles V and the 20th anniversary of the publication of its normative, anti-Philippist interpretation in *The Book of Concord.*

The Man—*Alter Philippus?*

The great question attaching to the life of David Chytraeus is the nature of his relationship to Philip Melanchthon. In the case of Andreae and Chemnitz their contemporaries did not doubt that they were on different wave lengths from that of the Wittenberg Biblical humanist. Chytraeus' relationship to Melanchthon, however, cannot be so easily dismissed, since he too was a Biblical humanist every inch of the way. His Biblical commentaries stand as a monument to his determination to declericalize the Scriptures and to make them an object of intense investigation by the clergy and educated laity alike. At the same time his extensive literary output as a historian served notice that he had that curiosity about man which was characteristic of the humanists. But in spite of his Melanchthonian penchants he was theologically speaking not a Philippist.

Evidence that Chytraeus was his own kind of Lutheran is the ecumenical significance he accorded the Augsburg Confession as he worked toward church reunification in Austria while at the same time resisting the ecclesiastical power politics exercised by the establishment there. Corroborating evidence is furnished by his bifurcated attitude toward the Formula of Concord, an attitude which on the one hand recognized the Formula's orthodoxy and on the other hand impugned its use as an instrument whereby consciences might be tortured. One might also cite his doctrine of "certainty," which in its main thrust is Lutheran but which cannot resist muddying the waters by supplying some supports for theological certainty made out of the clay bricks of humanist philosophy. Yet Chytraeus himself sensed that these arguments were not convincing and that only God could vouchsafe divine certainty to a person. [73]

It was this divine certainty which on the day of his death Chytraeus desired and received. As he felt the hour of his redemption approaching, he made an earnest confession of his sins and received the *cibus viatorum,* the sacramental food for the wayfarer on his pilgrimage to the world to come. Thereupon he said: "Now we are, praise God, well-secured." [74] On the wall over his bed there was hanging a picture of the crucified Jesus under which Chytraeus had in his own hand written the seven words from the cross. His family and colleagues surrounded his bed and comforted him with the promises of Holy Scripture, to which he responded "Amen" until shortly before midnight, at which time he fell softly and quietly into his final sleep without having tasted the bitterness of death.[75]

His body was laid to rest on June 29, the festival of St. Peter and St. Paul the Apostles, in the "Jakobskirche," where this great lay theologian of the Lutheran Church had so regularly worshiped during the almost 50 years of his Christian service to the Rostock University community. His colleague and friend, Superintendent Lucas Bakmeister, preached on the Gospel for the festival, Matt. 16:13-19. And a joyous festival it was indeed for this "alterum Philippum" who in life and in death stood on that ecumenical confession of Peter and Paul, the patron saints of Catholicism and Protestantism respectively: "You are the Christ, the Son of the living God."[76]

NIKOLAUS SELNECKER
—THE WEATHER VANE?

The original "St. Nikolaus" (ca. 280—ca. 350) was sometimes called the "Boy Bishop" because of his youth at the time he was appointed bishop of Myra in Asia Minor. His 16th-century Lutheran namesake, Nikolaus Selnecker, was born on his festival day in the year 1530. Although Selnecker did not become the Lutheran equivalent of a bishop (superintendent) until he was a mature 38 years of age, he did become the "Boy Organist" at the age of 12 in the castle chapel of the thriving city of Nuernberg. And though he never developed a reputation, as did his patron saint, for working miracles and for generous deeds especially among children, he enjoyed the task of giving instruction to members of the boys' choir in Dresden and then helping to develop the famous boys' Motet Choir, later associated with J. S. Bach, at St. Thomas' Church in Leipzig. Whether Selnecker was a bold confessor as was his namesake, who participated in the Council of Nicaea, or whether he was a weather vane, as some of his contemporaries tagged him, responding to the direction of whatever theological wind was blowing—these are questions which must be considered as we look at the child who was father of the man.

The Child[1]

Selnecker was born at Hersbruck (about 16 miles east-northeast of Nuernberg) to upper middle class parents. His father was the town clerk and notary public there, but while Nikolaus was still a child he moved the family to Nuernberg to seek fame and fortune, and he soon became the chief clerical administrator of that flourishing city. In this position he became friends with Melanchthon and Veit Dietrich and also was respected by Emperor Charles V and King Ferdinand. It was natural that he would desire a good education for his two sons, the elder, Georg, by his first wife, and the younger, Nikolaus, by his second wife. Georg studied theology and eventually became a pastor in Schwabach. Nikolaus was destined by his father to become a jurist, but a higher destiny intervened and he too studied theology. Beforehand, however, he devoted himself to a humanistic education in the well-staffed *Gymnasium* in Nuernberg. At the same time his theological interests were stimulated by W. Link, Veit Dietrich, and others, whose sermons he not only heard attentively but would then study on the basis of his own stenographic notes.[2]

At age 19 (1549) Nikolaus was about to leave home for Wittenberg and its famous university, but God intervened in his life through an event which Satan meant for evil but God meant for good. He was ambushed by a tramp named Schlappenhauer, who shot and nearly fatally wounded him. For months he was bedridden, and an entire year passed before he could take up his studies at Wittenberg. The incident seemed permanently to have weakened his body, and he was frequently ill thereafter. Psychologically his self-assurance was shaken. But God used this experience to create in Selnecker a deep piety that hungered for the comfort and steadfastness which the promises of God alone could give. Thus, for example, his naturally musical and poetic spirit learned to derive its inspiration from the Spirit-breathed promises of Holy Scripture, and instead of selling his musical talent to the emperor, as well he might have, he brought it as a living sacrifice to his Lord Jesus and as a ministry to Christ's body, the church.[3]

When Selnecker arrived in Wittenberg in 1550, he was not without a point of friendly personal contact. The fact that his father was a personal friend of Melanchthon had the effect of opening the door of the great scholar's home to Nikolaus, who moved in about the time that David Chytraeus moved out.[4] Melanchthon in a letter to Selnecker's father once praised the young man's "genius, modesty, and piety."[5] Though the father still envisioned a legal career for his son, Melanchthon soon recognized his deeply religious nature and theological bent and encouraged him along these lines. After receiving his master's degree in 1554, Selnecker devoted himself enthusiastically to the study of theology with such teachers as Bugenhagen, Georg Major, Joh. Foerster, Paul Eber, and of course Melanchthon himself. It was during these years under the influence of the great Biblical humanist that Selnecker's irenic character was strongly reinforced and he became convinced of the essential consensus between Luther and Melanchthon and of the importance of a consensus among all Lutherans. He later wrote that he considered it one of the greatest treasures of his life "that I had the opportunity to have the one and only Philip as a teacher, to hear him, almost daily to associate with him, to speak with him and consult with him."[6]

While pursuing theological studies at Wittenberg, Selnecker simultaneously began to hold lectures as a *Privatdocent*. He covered a considerable range of subjects, dealing with dialectic and rhetoric, Aristotle's *On the Soul*, Acts, Romans, Matthew, and Melanchthon's *Examen ordinandorum*. Apparently the 25-year-old Selnecker was attractive as a lecturer to the youth of his day, since it is reported that 200 of them were crowding into his classroom. But the relative security enjoyed while "doing theology" in an academic setting was a situation that ended abruptly when, as a result of the recommendation of Melanchthon, Selnecker received and accepted a call as third court chaplain in Dresden, the residence of Elector August of Saxony. After being ordained to the holy ministry in Wittenberg on the Festival of Epiphany and bidding farewell to the university there by an address characteristically expressing his uncertainty, namely, "On Preferring Academic Life to Life at the Court," he left for Dresden and began his work there in January of 1558.

Within a year's time Selnecker was given an additional assignment which he gladly accepted. A vacancy had developed in the position of the instructor to members of the boys' choir, and since Selnecker had a flair for music the invitation to work with the members of the choir was a welcome one. About this same time he also received the special assignment from "Father August" and "Mother Anna" of supervising the education of the six-year-old electoral prince, Alexander. When in 1565 Alexander died, he was remembered for his piety, a piety which Selnecker, no doubt, had done much to nourish as he attempted to carry out Elector August's orders: "I am determined that the prince should become a 'Doctor of the Catechism.'"[7]

Selnecker's star seemed to be shining brightly. "Mother Anna" particularly liked his preaching. He was making his mark at the court. And he fell in love with Margaretha, daughter of the superintendent at Dresden, Daniel Greiser.[8] So in 1559 he married and established his own household.[9] But already dark clouds were forming in the sky of Selnecker's fortune. Later he wrote:

> While I was still independent and unordained, nothing seemed to be beyond my grasp; at one time I considered becoming a knight and entering the lists. But after I was called into the pastoral office I was put to school and learned: I am nothing.[10]

The Father

Already as a "child" Selnecker had had to face the uncertainties provoked by the imminence of death. The thought of the following hymn stanza was refined in the crucible of his own experience:

> O Lord, my God, I cry to Thee;
> In my distress Thou helpest me.
> My soul and body I commend
> Into Thy hands; Thine angel send
> To guide me home and cheer my heart
> When Thou dost call me to depart.[11]

This faith of the "child" was now to be tested as the "father" carried out the ministry to which he had been called at the electoral court in Dresden.

Selnecker spent about seven years in Dresden at this time, years rich in theological productivity as well as pastoral experience. A glance at the variety of his scholarly publications during this period might prompt one to the erroneous conclusion that he had withdrawn from his practical pastoral responsibilities and was simply devoting himself to the quiet life of the scholar. His literary activity touched upon all areas of interest to the well-informed theologian of his day, e. g.:

Philosophy—an epitome of Aristotle's *Physics* (1561)
O.T. Exegesis—Proverbs (1558); Psalms (1563)
N.T. Exegesis—Johannine Epistles (1561)
Church History—a catalog of the chief church councils from the time of the apostles to the present (1564)
Systematic Theology—a study on man's fall and on the structure of human institutions (1560); two pamphlets on the Lord's Supper (1561); a study on the providence of God (1564)
Practical Theology—a versified catechism (1562); a book on catechetical methodology (1564).[12]

But his work as a scholar did not mean his withdrawal from that arena where any theology must be tested—the people of God gathered around Word and sacraments. Selnecker's preaching brought forth responses, both positive and negative. The elector and his wife both responded with enthusiasm, and it was Selnecker, rather than one of his superiors, who was chosen to deliver the memorial sermon on the occasion of the death of King Christian of Denmark, father of "Mother Anna." It was also Selnecker whom the electoral couple chose to accompany them to Berlin (1560) to celebrate the marriage of Duke Julius of Brunswick to Princess Hedwig of Brandenburg. Yet Selnecker was also able to draw a vigorously negative response to his sermons, especially when he touched upon the sins of those in high places.

Before recounting the particular incident which was related to Selnecker's release from his duties at Dresden, it would be well to note the influence his father-in-law, Daniel Greiser, had in coloring his personality. Basically Selnecker was a somewhat anxious though irenic spirit with a poet's sensitivities and deep feelings. Greiser, on the other hand, was a man of commanding personality who was convinced that the only way to deal with opposition was with stronger opposition. Selnecker had with some trepidation left the relative safety of academia for the hurly-burly of life at court, so it was undoubtedly with great admiration that he observed the boldness with which Greiser handled himself in this milieu. But admiration soon turned to imitation and thus to a coloring of his personality which was not always to stand him in good stead.[13] Only in the school of adversity would he continually learn to pray:

> Oh, keep us in Thy Word, we pray;
> The guile and rage of Satan stay!
> Oh, may Thy mercy never cease!
> Give concord, patience, courage, peace.[14]

At any rate the tone of Selnecker's sermons at Dresden slowly began to give more and more evidence of Greiser's influence, and the discordant climax came in the following way. Because of an illness Selnecker's place in the pulpit of the Castle Church was taken one Sunday by the first preacher of Dresden's "Frauenkirche," a certain Martin Hofmann. The latter was at the moment agitated by the fact that his poverty-stricken mother had lost her grain harvest as a result of damage done by wild game which was protected for the benefit of the hunting parties enjoyed by the nobility. So Hofmann took his chance when preaching in the Castle Church to get off a few good shots at the nobility assembled there. They, however, did not appreciate being sitting ducks for Hofmann's blasts and so forbade him the use of such immoderate speech from the pulpit. He responded that they were speaking like the worldly wise and that he would not desist since the Word of God was to have free course in convicting the world of sin. For this Hofmann was "invited" to leave town, which he did on the very day of the investigation. Meanwhile Selnecker had returned to his pulpit and began to fire away at the same target. Whereas Hofmann had cited Jesus' words "It is not fair to take the children's bread and throw it to the dogs" against the nobility, Selnecker went so far as to say that if this abuse did not cease "the nobility and their servants would go to the devil."[15] This was Selnecker the son-in-law of Greiser speaking, rather than Selnecker the student and former house companion of Melanchthon.

When called upon to justify his outspoken language, Selnecker said:

> If we were still living under a pre-Christian government, we would have to endure such and similar temporal hardships without recourse until God Himself should intervene, and in addition we would gladly and sincerely have to thank God that we have His Word which we can preach, hear, and learn. But since we are living under a Christian government, which has God's Word in its truth and purity, there is all the more reason to expect mercy. However, my only advice is this, that pious subjects acknowledge their sin and devoutly pray that God Himself would enlighten our lord's heart, spirit, and mind, thus that Your Grace would recognize the office laid upon you by God and that we under your protection might lead a quiet and peaceful life.[16]

This is language once again more consistent with the spirit of Melanchthon.

In answer to the charge that he had given the elector over to Satan, Selnecker responded: "It is my desire to snatch souls out of the jaws of the devil and in no way to deliver them to him, particularly not the soul of a Christian potentate who is an administrator and renewer of the church of Christ Jesus." Since he was accused of doing in public what he should have done, if at all, only in private, he said that he had no choice, one reason being that he was not the elector's father-confessor. But in a surprisingly bold vein he then continued:

> In the first place it is undeniably true that my gracious lord has through his frequent hunting neglected and relegated to second place the office which God has given and commended to his care. . . . Every Christian ruler should daily consider these two points—
> 1) Who has placed him in this high office, i.e., from whom has he received it;
> 2) Why has he been given such an office and position. . . . Neither do I wish to deny that on several occasions when I myself was accompanying the hunt, the following question occurred to me— whether I, who have been designated a teacher of God's Word, ought with a good conscience be thus involved, since it could happen that such riding about could lead to the neglect by my gracious lord of his

high and godly office, and no one of us who is concerned with God's will and command can excuse and sanction that.

This written statement to the elector Selnecker then signed and added: "Lord Christ, Yours be the honor, the praise, and the glory. More I cannot."[17] The stakes were not as high as for Luther at Worms, but in its own way this was a Worms for Selnecker. His conscience was bound by the Word of God, and there was a price to pay. He spent the rest of his life learning to pay it—and in singing:

> A trusty weapon is Thy Word,
> Thy church's buckler, shield, and sword.
> Oh, let us in its power confide
> That we may seek no other guide![18]

Actually there were also other pressures developing against Selnecker in Dresden, pressures resulting more from his doctrinal position than from his pastoral practice. Already in 1561 he had participated in a theological consultation at Dresden on the Lord's Supper. His contribution made it clear to men like Caspar Peucer (1525—1602; doctor of medicine; son-in-law of Melanchthon) and Georg Cracow (1525—75; professor of jurisprudence in Wittenberg, privy counselor in Dresden) that Selnecker could not be counted on to flatten Luther's doctrine to fit the dimensions of Calvin's theology. And so these Crypto-Calvinists, as they were called, planned to hasten Selnecker's departure from Dresden. The events surrounding the confrontation between Selnecker and the elector on the issue of the latter's hunting presented them with an inviting pretext to encourage the elector to accept Selnecker's resignation. Elector August did dismiss him politely with instruction to consider another position elsewhere in Electoral Saxony. That Selnecker saw his departure tied to the scheming of the Crypto-Calvinists seems apparent from his farewell sermon, preached on the basis of Ps. 141:9—"Keep me from the trap which they have laid for me, and from the snares of evildoers."[19] Nevertheless he left in a spirit of good will and penned the following farewell poem:

> Against no soul hold I a thing,
> Instead a song of thanks I sing.
> We patient wait and suffer much,
> Until in death our goal we touch.
> Our faith and conscience free from guilt
> With joy upon the Rock is built.[20]

Selnecker had in mind to return to his native Nuernberg, but before this materialized he received offers from two of Germany's leading conservative universities, Jena in Saxony and Tuebingen in Wuerttemberg, the latter call perhaps through the instrumentality of Tuebingen's troubleshooting chancellor, Jakob Andreae.[21] Selnecker chose to accept the invitation to become professor of theology in Jena (1565). Since, however, Elector August had just recently deposed the ultraconservative Flacian party from Jena, the new faculty was Philippist in its leaning. When in 1567 Duke Johann Wilhelm assumed leadership in Ernestine Saxony, restoring representatives of the Flacian party to the professorships in Jena, Selnecker was deposed along with and by virtue of his association with the Philippists. The latter had difficulty abiding Selnecker because of his Lutheranism, whereas the Flacians would have no truck with him since he seemed willing to negotiate with the Philippists. So within two years Selnecker was again jobless, not for reasons seeming to indicate that he was a theological weather vane but because in vain he stood for reconciling what others refused to hope could be reconciled. So bitterly was he resisted by the Flacians that they nicknamed the hapless Selnecker "Seelhenker," i. e., "Soul Executioner."[22]

Elector August had by this time overcome any bad feelings he may have had about Selnecker, and he saw to it that his former court chaplain received the appointment as professor of theology at the University of Leipzig (1568), a position which had just been vacated by the Philippist Viktorin Strigel (1524—69).[23] In addition Selnecker was also named pastor of St. Thomas' Church and superintendent of Leipzig. As professor he lectured on Melanchthon's *Loci* and defended the church of Electoral Saxony against the attacks of the Flacians issuing out of Jena. He published a commentary on Genesis, which he dedicated to Elector August with a declaration of his agreement with the *Corpus Philippicum*.[24] Soon after his arrival he received a visit from Jakob Andreae, who had been authorized by Duke Julius of Brunswick to invite Selnecker to assist with the reformation of the church of Brunswick. This invitation plus a second from Emperor Maximilian II to conduct the organization of the Evangelical churches in Austria he for the time being turned down for reasons of health. Two years later (1570), however, he accepted on a two-year basis the offer from Duke Julius to assume the office of court preacher and general superintendent at Wolfenbuettel.[25]

Before assuming this new though temporary office, Selnecker followed the wishes of Elector August by obtaining his doctor's degree

(1570) from the University of Wittenberg. In this connection he participated with other doctoral candidates in a public disputation which, as it turned out, brought him under suspicion by his new colleagues in Brunswick-Wolfenbuettel, Jakob Andreae and Martin Chemnitz. The point at issue was a thesis concerning the "personal union" of the two natures of Christ and the so-called "communication of attributes." Andreae and Chemnitz felt that the thesis defended at Wittenberg stood in contradiction to the recently arrived-at agreement at Zerbst and that it consequently was a violation of sound Lutheran teaching.[26] Accordingly Duke Julius commissioned Selnecker to report these matters to Elector August in Dresden for the purpose of effecting a satisfactory resolution of the opposing positions. Upon his return to Wolfenbuettel, Selnecker had in hand a document which Andreae thought was certain to be the foundation of a consensus between the contending Evangelical churches. Selnecker himself later said of it: "I returned with a document which was sound in what it said but slippery in what it did not say; I so wanted to put the best construction on everything and to be left with no suspicions at all even if I should test it all out personally."[27] However, when the Wittenberg theologians got wind of the claims being made by Andreae and Selnecker, they quickly disavowed that they had conceded anything.

The incident only seemed to reactivate Selnecker's uncertainty syndrome alluded to above. He came into conflict with Chemnitz until he agreed not to support the introduction of the *Corpus Philippicum* and until he recognized as his own the position of Chemnitz on the so-called "multivolipresence" as described by Chemnitz in his extensive monograph *De duabus naturis in Christo*, a book Selnecker referred to as "magnificent."[28] On the other hand he entered into a literary exchange with the Philippists, particularly on questions surrounding the interpretation of Acts 3:20 f.[29] His capacity for appeasement was expressed again in the so-called "Dresden Consensus" (1571), a statement on the doctrine of the Lord's Supper which Selnecker considered sound, a position which others thought once again betrayed him as a theological weather vane.[30] The cloud of suspicion which he sensed was hanging over him in Wolfenbuettel prompted him on one occasion to write Elector August that he "would gladly crawl back to Dresden from Wolfenbuettel on all fours."[31] The elector was sympathetic and sent him a letter in which he encouraged Selnecker to suffer patiently and leave his vindication to God, whose cause he was defending.[32]

In 1572 the Gnesio-Lutheran Timotheus Kirchner was summoned

from Jena by Duke Julius to assume the position of general superintendent at Wolfenbuettel. To avoid theological friction between Kirchner and Selnecker, the latter took up residence in nearby Gandersheim, the location of Duke Julius' recently founded academy, at which Selnecker then also began to give instruction in theology.[33] During this time he found he could escape the depressions he experienced as a result of the *rabies theologorum* by immersing himself in scholarly activity, and the product of this labor was his major work in systematic theology, the *Institutio religionis Christianae*. He dedicated it to Duke Ludwig of Wuerttemberg and wrote in the preface of his great joy that there was such a unanimity of doctrine between the churches of Lower Saxony and Wuerttemberg.[34] His final contribution to the reformation of Duke Julius' land was the introduction of a Lutheran church order in Oldenburg (1573). While still there, he received a summons from Elector August to return to Saxony to again take up his theological professorship in Leipzig. Here he would enter into the mature period of his life after having been strengthened in his Lutheran convictions through his contact with Chemnitz. Yet even now he was not so much a strong party man as he was a man who fled to Christ in the face of party strife.[35]

The Man—Florens

Selnecker did not exactly leap at the opportunity to return to Leipzig. He had begun to feel at home in the vigorously Lutheran climate of Lower Saxony, and he sensed that to return to Leipzig was to enter once again into the midst of "leones et lupos."[36] But after a period of uncertainty and soul searching he accepted Elector August's offer, and on Feb. 1, 1574, he delivered his inaugural address, his second as a professor at Leipzig. His mind now seemed made up to see it through, for when soon after he received a call to become professor at the newly established University of Helmstedt[37] he turned it down, choosing to live by the prayer he had penned while in Wolfenbuettel:

> Let me be Thine forever,
> Thou faithful God and Lord;
> From Thee let nothing drive me,
> Hold me close to Thy Word.
> Lord, do not let me waver,
> But give me steadfastness,
> And for such grace forever
> Thy holy name I'll bless.[38]

These words became his daily prayer, and the world was soon to witness how a faithful God honored this prayer of faith.

Selnecker was about to engage in the most significant activity of his career—the activity surrounding the composition and implementation of the Formula of Concord. The particular event leading up to this possibility was the recognition by Elector August that the Philippistic doctrine he had been protecting in his territory against the attacks of the Flacians actually did depart from Luther's teaching. This revelation came to the elector in 1574 upon the publication of the so-called *Exegesis perspicua*, a document produced by the Philippists and one in which they far less cryptically than was their custom professed a theological position much closer to Calvin than to Luther.[39] Selnecker was one of the first to respond to this document, and he did so with a statement on the Lord's Supper which clearly identified him with Luther, the Unaltered Augsburg Confession, and the position taken by the leading churches of Lower Saxony. He also recognized the weakness in the "Torgau Confession" (1574), which though plainly upholding the Lutheran teaching still assumed a doctrinal agreement between Melanchthon and Luther.[40]

It was thus practically overnight that Elector August emerged as the new political leader most desperate and eager to effect a union of all genuine Lutherans through a clarification of the issues. To this end the Wuerttemberg court preacher Lucas Osiander (1534—1604) and the Stuttgart provost Balthasar Bidembach (1533—78) were commissioned (1575) to prepare a document that would clearly and simply set forth the Lutheran position as a measure for testing doctrinal orthodoxy. Known as the "Maulbronn Formula" (after Cloister Maulbronn, located about 20 miles east of Karlsruhe), it served as an important tool in the hands of Andreae as he negotiated toward the settlement later achieved at Torgau.[41] Of interest here are the circumstances leading to Andreae's coming into the employ of Elector August and how Selnecker played into those circumstances.

Early in 1576 Elector August convened his theologians at Lichtenberg (about 20 miles northeast of Dresden) for the purpose of sizing up where each stood and determining a course of action for establishing peace in the church. Selnecker emerged as a leading figure at this convention, as his motion to undo the official status clinging to the "Wittenberg Catechism," the "Dresden Consensus," and the *Corpus Philippicum* was carried. In their place he recommended the adoption of a new *corpus doctrinae* more Lutheran in character, and he also advised that the electors and princes arrange a convention of such representative theologians as, e. g., Chytraeus, Chemnitz, Andreae, and Marbach to discuss the doctrinal differences. In this way Selnecker was instrumental in prompting Elector August to call Andreae to Saxony as his special adviser in matters dealing with church union.[42]

When Andreae arrived in Saxony, Elector August received him at Torgau (April 1576) and carefully listened to his plans and recommendations as to the relative merits of the "Swabian-Saxon Concord" and the "Maulbronn Formula."[43] The elector then followed the proposal made by Selnecker at Lichtenberg and summoned the Lichtenberg theologians plus Chemnitz, Chytraeus, Musculus, and Koerner to Torgau to work out a confessional position. Almost against their most sanguine expectations the deliberations breathed a spirit of unity, with only the stormy Musculus providing any static.[44] Andreae, however, conducted the meetings so diplomatically that within 10 days (May 28—June7) the "Torgau Book" was ready to be presented to Elector August, who meanwhile had been supporting the deliberations with his earnest prayers. The conference participants were almost ecstatic that God should have shown them such mercy. Selnecker, whose original Lichtenberg proposal had now been actualized at Torgau, was asked to preach the sermon at the festive thanksgiving service which marked the conclusion of the conference.[45]

Shortly after the Torgau meeting Selnecker was reappointed as pastor of St. Thomas' Church and superintendent of Leipzig, positions he had held before going to Wolfenbuettel. It was Andreae who installed him into his office as superintendent (June 17, 1576), and from all appearances the relationship between the two men continued to be very cordial.[46] Both were passionate in their desire for Lutheran unity, and it was in their present positions that each made the most important contribution of his career.

Thus it was that Selnecker became one of the "Big Three" who met at Bergen Abbey in March of 1577 to consider the many critiques that were being registered in connection with the gaining of signatures for the "Torgau Book."[47] It is of interest to note that it was the same triumvirate, Andreae, Chemnitz, and Selnecker, that seven years earlier had been at work in Brunswick-Wolfenbuettel making the first tentative moves toward effecting unity among Lutherans.[48] If earlier in his life Selnecker had appeared to be beset by uncertainties, the years in Leipzig between 1574 and 1580 seemed to give notice of a man who had found himself and therewith also a certainty and self-confidence he had previously known only sporadically. He helped see the "Torgau Book" through to its revised form as the "Bergic Book" (May 29, 1577)[49] and then found himself appointed by Elector August to a commission, consisting also of Andreae and Polycarp Leyser (1552—1610), which had as its purpose the drumming up of committed support for the "Bergic Book" in Electoral Saxony. But beneath the surface certainty there struggled ever yet within Selnecker's psyche the "I" of the flesh and the "I" of the Spirit. The struggle surfaced particularly in his relation to Andreae, which Selnecker found strained beginning with the Torgau meeting of 1576 but which he repressed until 1579 when he shared his feelings with Elector August's wife, "Mother Anna," who as early as 1559 seemed to provide Selnecker the security that comes with a mother's acceptance.[50] On May 16, 1579, he wrote the "First Lady" of Saxony:

> I cannot keep it a secret from Your Grace that I am disturbed anew not only by the popular rumor that my gracious elector is supposedly irritated with me, but with the fact that Dr. Jakob has repeatedly issued threats against me as to how he intends to drive a wedge between me and my gracious lord. Up until now I've been inclined to let him make his attacks and to let the Lord Christ speak for me— something I still intend to do. But since I also recognize that the man is of no use to the churches and schools of this land, yea rather that he is highly dangerous and that he will only cause more damage the longer he remains here (since I also recognize, thank God, that my report can no longer do damage to the common task of establishing a *concordia,* something which until now I have always feared), I make bold to submit to Your Grace, and no longer to repress, this brief account and record of my observations on Dr. Jakob and to ask that Your Grace be pleased to hear it read by someone, as for example by Master Listenius, and then to do with it as Your Grace sees fit, namely, whether to give it also to my gracious lord or not. O God, how this offense hurts me, sapping all my strength and making me sick. But okay—may God settle it to His glory![51]

What were the facts behind Selnecker's defensive attitude over against Andreae?[52] This much seems to be clear. Andreae was looked upon as a foreign intruder by those in high places in the government of Elector August. Whereas Andreae wished to introduce into Saxony a highly centralized church organization similar to that operating in his home territory of Wuerttemberg, church officials in Electoral Saxony seemed to be jealous of prerogatives already theirs and were threatened by the possibility of losing these should Andreae's plans be implemented by the elector. When Andreae proposed a "superconsistory," it was difficult for Selnecker not to feel snubbed. The gorge of uncertainty began again to rise in his throat alongside his daily prayer:

> Let me be Thine forever,
> Thou faithful God and Lord . . . .[53]

There is no doubt that God proved faithful to Selnecker, and this in the face of Selnecker's own lack of faith as it became evident in the trumped-up charges he brought against his erstwhile ally and fellow concordist Andreae. The latter's slate was far from clean, as Chemnitz and Chytraeus were also more than ready to attest, but they appeared able to cope with their negative feelings about Andreae in a way less offensive than did Selnecker.[54]

When Andreae was taking hurt leave of Saxony, he stopped at Leipzig in order to reconcile himself with Selnecker as a Christian brother. Unfortunately Selnecker was not at home, so Andreae left him a note, dated New Year's Eve 1580. He wrote in conclusion:

> I pray good God that He grant you a right and true repentance and acknowledgement of this sin and that He not reserve you this grave temptation for your deathbed hour but that He preserve you from all evil. This is my heartfelt wish for you rather than that because of the circumstances I should take leave of you simply rushing by unnoticed. Instead I wish to take Christian leave of you as I did of His Grace's court preachers and consistorial theologians and thus demonstrate myself as a Christian in relation to you. Accordingly I all the more with joyful heart and unscathed conscience take off for Tuebingen to my dear wife, children, church, and school after having suffered long enough in these parts, and from my heart I wish for you that you superintend the churches and schools of this land in such a way as is pleasing to God in heaven.[55]

In a letter of defense which Andreae addressed to Elector August from Tuebingen (Aug. 22, 1581) he wrote:

> The chief reason behind Selnecker's break with me and his alliance with my opponents is this, as has been reported to me by trustworthy people: After he noticed that I was being opposed on all sides and that rumor had it that he alone sided with me, as was attested by his presence with us at all the conferences, his wife and children together with his father-in-law and close friends counseled him and called to

his attention that he should be careful with whom he associated, for I was a foreigner, would not be staying in the land, and thereafter everything would be blamed on him; accordingly he should disassociate himself from me before it was too late. This he also did without any valid reason.[56]

If Selnecker thought Andreae's dismissal would assure his own security, he was to be sorely disappointed. Nevertheless he enjoyed a relative security as long as his patrons, Elector August and Mother Anna, lived. During this time he was frequently engaged in defending the Formula of Concord. In 1581 he met with Chemnitz and Kirchner at Erfurt to produce the "Apology of the Formula of Concord." The following year he completed an improved Latin translation of the Formula and of the Smalcald Articles. In 1583 he participated in the disappointing Colloquy of Quedlinburg,[57] and the next year he produced a new edition of *The Book of Concord* with an improved text of the Unaltered Augsburg Confession. The year 1585 found him negotiating with the still-imprisoned Peucer (Elector August was taking no chances with the plotters of a new Crypto-Calvinist takeover),[58] but then in 1586 Elector August died (Mother Anna preceded him in death in 1585) and Selnecker's fate lay in the balance. August was succeeded by his son Christian I, whom as a child Selnecker "frequently had held in his arms"[59] but who now as elector, influenced greatly by Chancellor Nickolas Crell (1550—1601), permitted the reestablishment of Crypto-Calvinism.[60] Selnecker's time of testing had come again.

And God was faithful. The man who had stooped so low to guarantee his self-image that he was willing to sacrifice the reputation of another, namely, Jakob Andreae, now put his self-image, his positions, and his life on the line:

> From Thee let nothing drive me,
> Hold me close to Thy Word . . . .[61]

Selnecker showed himself willing to be driven from the securities of the flesh rather than to be driven from the confession of the God who was faithful to him in Christ as known to him in the Formula of Concord. In spite of the warnings coming to him from Dresden that he desist attacking Crell's ecclesiastical policies from the pulpit and with the pen, he carried on. In 1587 he published his great work *Christliche Psalmen, Lieder, und Kirchengesaenge*.[62] On May 17, 1589, he was met in the sacristy of

St. Thomas' Church, where he had worked so effectively for the past 15 years, by the official bearers of the announcement of his dismissal. Shorn of his ecclesiastical offices, he moved into a private home in Leipzig and proceeded to carry on a ministry through his literary activity. But soon this was also forbidden him, and in order to escape a prison sentence he fled to Halle and thence to Magdeburg, where he was received by friends. There in exile he prayed:

> Not age, not sickness drove me out unheard;
> It was, Lord Christ, your Sacrament and Word.
> Because I stood against a doctrine calcified,
> Therefore they drove me from my land and pride;
> In You alone, O Lord, then can I hide.[63]

What Selnecker had dared to lose rather than to deny his Lord he now received back in double measure. Early in 1590 he received two calls, the one to Hildesheim, the other to Brunswick-Lueneburg. He accepted the call to Hildesheim and served there as superintendent for about two years. During this time he was honored by invitations to assist with church administrative affairs in Wolfenbuettel, East Frisia, Minden, and Augsburg. In Hildesheim he preached frequently and held lectures on the Augsburg Confession. While his body was growing steadily weaker as a result of his exertions maintained even in times of serious illness, his confessional rigor grew stronger, although some have considered it a sign of mental *rigor mortis* when in resisting Calvinists he dammed them along with Jews and Turks.[64] A poetic soul, as was Luther, what he felt, he felt passionately, even and especially in death.

The Man—In Exitu

When Christian I of Electoral Saxony died in 1591, Crypto-Calvinism once again came under condemnation. During the regency of Duke Frederick William, who acted as guardian of Christian II, Lutheranism was reestablished, Crell and other Calvinists being imprisoned in the fortress at Koenigstein. Symbolic of the new regime's intentions was the invitation extended to Selnecker to return to Leipzig and to the offices he had there been forced to relinquish. When the call came, it found Selnecker in an advanced stage of failing health. Despite the urging of his friends not to accept while in such poor physical condition, Selnecker was not to be dissuaded. He considered this call to be the sixth of those he had accepted, and consequently mused:

> The seventh call will make me then
> In yonder life a citizen.[65]

The journey from Hildesheim to Leipzig required 11 days, and during this time Selnecker grew so weak that his traveling companions pleaded with him to make a halt long enough to recover his strength. But Selnecker sensed death to be knocking at his door and he wished to die in Leipzig, where he had labored to keep the evangelical water of life uncontaminated by Calvinistic impurities. Arriving in Leipzig he was immediately put to bed—the bed from which he would not rise again. Five days later on the Feast of the Holy Trinity (May 24, 1592) his end was upon him. A dark cloud threw its shadow over his soul as he cried out in anguish: "Must a man always be engulfed in a struggle while on this earth?"[66] At hand to comfort this reluctant "soldier" of the cross were the theologians Hunnius, Mirus, and Mylius. They asked him: "Are you ready to die on the basis of the doctrine which for so many years you have joyfully confessed?" He bowed his head deeply and answered the question with a broken but joyful "Yes." A quiet peace then surrounded him and he died. Two days later with great honor his mortal remains were buried in St. Thomas' Church, where to this day the voices of the famous "Thomanerchor" echo the Bach Cantatas, the sentiment of which Selnecker had done much to influence.[67]

The brazen plate which marks his grave accords him the title:

"Most illustrious Doctor, a very resolute defender of the testament of Christ."

He himself had prepared the following inscription, in verse, as was his wont:

> Though short I was, I now am tall; and had till now
> To live midst fallen world, so now to Thee, O Lord!
> Sick am I of this world and of its evil, how!
> So will I now in Jesus' arms eternity record.[68]

The memorial sermon was delivered by Prof. Georg Mylius, who said:

> In matters dealing with the teaching of the Christian religion he was not a weather vane or rubber neck; he was not like a reed shaken by the wind nor a man clothed in soft raiment who for the sake of royal favor and worldly honor would let himself be moved to change his religious convictions; nay rather he remained even to the grave fast and immovable in the truth, once he had come to know it and confess it.[69]

The Man—In Memoriam

"Not a weather vane or a rubber neck." So Georg Mylius at Selnecker's funeral. But others felt differently, as for instance, Jakob Andreae.[70] Yet when it came to the crunch, Selnecker, who like John the Baptist wrestled with his own version of the question, "Are you[Luther] he who is to come, or shall we look for another [Calvin]," was prepared to put his head on the block. He was not proud of his own ability to stand firm, for he better than anyone knew his own weakness and confessed it when he prayed:

> Lord, do not let me waver,
> But give me steadfastness. . . .[71]

A perspective on the steadfastness of Selnecker's orthodoxy can be gained from a review of his sermons, especially those preached on the occasion of a burial—a time when a man's theology can easily be seen either to stand or fall. These sermons betray a pessimistic anthropology and an optimistic theology—a theology which is optimistic because it is Christocentric, as can be seen from the following example:

> Apart from Christ all learning and all worldly wisdom are unadulterated foolishness and poison in God's eyes. Apart from Christ all of man's virtues are nothing but sin and unrighteousness. For whatever is not of faith is sin. Apart from Christ all the works and the entire life and being of man are, when placed before God, unholy and an abomination, worthy of rejection and damnation. Apart from Christ man continues in sin and death, eternally under God's wrath, in the jaws and the power of Satan himself. All teaching, all piety or virtue, the entire life and death of every man who does not believe in Christ are completely, when we put the best construction on them, a stinking, perishable, proud, rotten boast of a miserable man sick with leprosy and a corruption of the soul and the body.[72]

Father Luther himself could hardly have said it more strongly.

Selnecker enjoyed citing Luther in his sermons. A characteristic reference would be the following:

> Luther asked a student whether he looked forward to his death and what he had in mind to bring God as a gift. The student answered that he was both willing and prepared to die and that he intended to offer God "a contrite heart, sprinkled with the blood of the Son of God." Thereupon Luther said: "To this end may the Lord Jesus Christ help you, for in bringing this you bring that which comprehends all good

and you will be an acceptable and welcome guest. God grant that all of us bring such a precious treasure with us. Then we will never be able to be turned aside or lost."[73]

The sacraments were for Selnecker a rich source of comfort in the face of death. He understood Baptism to be the means whereby we are united with Christ's death and resurrection, and of the Lord's Supper he said:

Oh, how rich a blessing comes from using the holy sacraments! They seal and strengthen us in the faith, and as surely as the words say "Given for you" and "Shed for you," so surely do they testify to and confirm our salvation. For how is it possible that he should be lost who with soul and body participates in the body and blood of Christ?[74]

On occasion the "gentle" Selnecker could roar with indignation. One wonders whether the indignation was righteous or not, whether it betrays self-assurance in Christ or self-doubt arising from the flesh:

Many a sow, many an Epicurean, many a grumble-hans slavers, slogs, and snorts around in our day about matters having to do with God, about the Person of Christ, about His holy Supper. At his best he is nothing in the eyes of the world but a detestable and beastly person. If he were to speak on the subject of gluttony, drunkenness, and sexual perversion, he would speak as an expert.[75]

It would be difficult to imagine these words coming from a man without convictions. No sentimental drivel from a moderating theologian here. Yet does a man with God-given convictions fight the Lord's battles with such verbal overkill rather than with "the whole armor of God" as described by the apostle Paul? Is this God's answer to Selnecker's prayer:

> Lord, do not let me waver,
> But give me steadfastness . . . ?

Allowing for the coarseness characteristic of 16th-century Germany, one nevertheless here detects a cover-up of Selnecker's lifelong battle with insecurity. It was a battle in which Selnecker through Christ indeed bruised the head of the serpent. But the bruise in the heel of his own flesh remained evident, as it does for us all, up to the grave.

Selnecker's legacy to the church has been most obviously appropriated in the area of hymnody. Many Lutherans in Europe, America, and beyond are still familiar with four of his hymns: "Lord Jesus Christ, with Us Abide"; "O Faithful God, Thanks Be to Thee"; "Let Me Be Thine Forever"; "O Lord, My God, I Cry to Thee"[76] Theologians dealing with the development of doctrinal terminology in the 16th century will be familiar with at least the following works by Selnecker: *Paedagogia christiana* (1566); *Institutio religionis christianae* (1573); *Notatio de studio theologiae* (1579); *Forma explicationis examinis ordinandorum* (1582). Also as an exegete Selnecker was no slouch. Among his writings in this area we have an interpretation of the three letters of John (1561), of the Psalter and nearly all the OT prophets, of the Revelation of John, of Genesis (1569), of the letters of Paul, and a harmony of the Gospels. In the area of history he wrote on the councils, Luther, the Augsburg Confession, and the Formula of Concord. And finally there are the numerous published sermons, giving us the picture of a man who was simultaneously a professor, a pastor, and a poet.

Selnecker had a compulsion to put his feelings into verse. Many of his publications are accompanied by examples of his poetry, much of which, however, would not be considered as meriting a great deal of praise. Yet he seemed to find something therapeutic in the practice of versifying. He identified readily with the authors of the Psalter, of which he wrote:

> Oh, how full of comfort and precious is the Psalter, for which I will thank God in all eternity. When I turn to it, my life is restored even though I have often been at the point of death and heaven and earth seemed to be closing in upon me. May a gracious God leave me only my little Psalter; for the rest He can take what He wills.[77]

Taken together, Selnecker's publications number about 175 (94 in Latin and 81 in German). This is astounding especially when one considers his own remark that during his entire professional career he never enjoyed general good health and also that for a period he was "secretly bothered by apparitions."[78] These seemed to be connected with the *rabies theologorum*, i.e., the experience of a party spirit which on the one hand would cry "I belong to Luther" and on the other "I belong to Melanchthon" (cf. 1 Cor. 1:10-13). On one occasion he complained:

> The devil is outshouting and outsinging David's entire chorus, and with his rattling and rapping he is ruining the smooth rhythm, the sweet flutes and cymbals, indeed often the entire work of those who love peace.[79]

Selnecker was at heart a peacemaker; and because he was, he appeared to some to be a weather vane. He was short in stature, which invited many a nickname and perhaps added to his feelings of insecurity, but he prayed his way through to strength and was ultimately honored as a bold and faithful confessor. One wonders what his feelings were when two years before his own death he heard of the passing of Andreae.[80] Perhaps like Peter he heard the crow of the cock and remembered the word of the Lord. Perhaps he prayed:

O faithful God, thanks be to Thee
Who dost forgive iniquity.
Thou grantest help in sin's distress,
And soul and body dost Thou bless.[81]

THE FORMULATORS
—OF CONCORD OR DISCORD?

Behind an investigation into the lives of the four chief formulators of the Formula of Concord lies a question which was succinctly captured in the Latin titles of two books written in the early decades of the 17th century. In 1607 the Calvinist Rudolf Hospinian published his *Concordia discors* ("Discordant Harmony"), which was followed in 1614 by a reply from the Lutheran Leonard Hutter entitled *Concordia concors* ("Concordant Harmony").[1] At issue was the question regarding the "fruit" of the Formula of Concord (and by implication the "fruit" of the lives of its four chief formulators). Did it produce a confessional choir singing a concordant or a discordant harmony? Did the formulators themselves contrive to produce a statement of concord whereas in reality they personified positions of discord? Perhaps the question is as misleading as if one should ask whether Jesus brought peace or the sword. Perhaps there is a peace which brings the sword and a sword which brings peace. At any rate there is a peace which is no peace, and we are concerned with determining whether the formulators of the Formula of Concord knew their limit and accordingly simply pointed us to the peace which the world cannot give but can only receive.

The initial hostility which Andreae's and Selnecker's efforts at formulating a concord received from Chemnitz and Chytraeus seems to indicate that especially the latter two were aware that there was a peace they could not give.[2] Yet in the end we find the four united at Torgau praising God for having done the impossible.[3] The miracle is underscored by the fact that the harmony held despite open personal animosity between Andreae and Chemnitz,[4] between Andreae and Selnecker,[5] between Chytraeus and the "Big Three,"[6] and between Chemnitz and Selnecker.[7] But the miracle itself is tarnished somewhat by the fact that vested interests cooperated with the Holy Spirit to effect it. Andreae seemed determined to father the concord no matter who the mother or how she was hurting.[8] And Chemnitz, Chytraeus, and Selnecker all preferred to bite their tongues for a longer or shorter period of time rather than endanger their own investment in the concord.[9]

The investment of each in the desired concord, however, was not all that was at stake. Each also had an investment in his past, including the relationship to his foremost teacher. In the case of Chemnitz, Chytraeus, and Selnecker this was Melanchthon. In Andreae's case it was Brenz. This presents us with the strange paradox that although Andreae never met Luther, whereas Chemnitz and Chytraeus did, Andreae could express his allegiance to Luther without counting the cost in terms of his relationship to Melanchthon, whereas the others could not. They all owed a personal debt of gratitude to Melanchthon as their teacher, and all had lived as guests in his house.[10] This, of course, meant that Melanchthon exercised far more influence on Chemnitz, Chytraeus, and Selnecker than he did on Andreae, who was beholden to Brenz, who was beholden to Luther and to his duke. As a result, while the three were both attracted and repelled by the *rabies theologorum*, Andreae moved to the beat of *pecca fortiter*, perhaps a bit too eagerly at times. Thus Andreae could exercise a single-mindedness about the *goal* of concordia which was difficult for the other three as long as they agonized more profoundly about the *basis* of concordia. Unfortunately Luther's boldness and Melanchthon's fastidiousness could both be misused for achieving political and/or personal goals, and some of this seems to have been at work to a greater or lesser degree in all four "concordia men."[11]

Another factor contributing to the concord/discord ambivalence was the attitude each of the formulators took relative to the "spirit of the times." This *Zeitgeist* has been termed "personalism," and by it is meant the integration of a person's subjective feelings and intentions with the objective and abstracted expressions of the person's commitment.[12] Luther the reformer and Erasmus the humanist both shared in this "spirit," but each in his own way. The reformer's "personalism" is summed up in his emphasis on the "for me" of the Gospel. The humanist's "personalism," on the other hand, could be characterized as the "for you" contained in a commitment to the attitude of toleration. The two positions need not and ought not be mutually exclusive, but they become so when the dynamic for the "for you" is located in man rather than in God as revealed in Jesus Christ. A contradiction also occurs when the "for me" of the Gospel does not transform the beneficiary into a "for you" kind of person, i.e., tolerant in the sense that the burden-assuming

Jesus was tolerant. It is of interest to observe how each of the formulators expresses himself on this question.

Andreae certainly understood himself as walking in the footsteps of Luther rather than of Erasmus. His life, like Luther's, was rooted in the "for me" of the Gospel. But a humanist would be justified in his query as to whether Andreae permitted the dynamic of this Gospel to transform a cultural characteristic of long standing, the spirit of nontoleration. The approach Andreae had taken on the occasion of the conversion of the Jew[13] and the method he later employed in implementing the Formula of Concord[14] would seem to indicate that the "for me" had great difficulty in transforming Andreae into a "for you" person.

There is a poignancy in Chemnitz' answer to the question. Like Andreae he too was totally committed to the "for me" of the Gospel. And like Andreae he too had difficulty in being transformed into a "for you" person, tending to rely instead on law, order, and the anathema directed against both false doctrine and immoral living as the means of assuring the ongoing presence of the Gospel's "for me" rather than giving the priority to becoming the lived expression of it in his relation to opponents of his position.[15] But toward the end of his life Chemnitz seemed to suffer the "crucifixion" that signaled the beginning of his own transformation. He risked his own security rather than blink at the misdemeanor of his duke,[16] and ultimately he died with a heavy heart as he sensed the discrepancy between the "for me" to which the Formula of Concord pointed and the failure of the quarreling theologians to exercise the "for you" among themselves.[17]

Of the four formulators the one who appeared to stand closest to the humanist tradition was Chytraeus. His particularly intimate relationship with Melanchthon was a result of their mutual commitment to humanist ideals. But both also shared Luther's commitment to the evangelical "for me." Although Chytraeus sensed that Melanchthon's evangelical witness had weaknesses, he preferred, like Thomas More, to suffer the consequences of the duplicity of silence rather than to deny the "for me" of the Gospel by failing to express a "for you" attitude toward his teacher Melanchthon, by whom in fact he had been confirmed in his own "for me" faith.[18] Thus in his attitude toward the Formula of Concord Chytraeus could endorse it as a valid expression of the evangelical "for me" but he could not in good conscience then deny that same confession by failing to exercise it through showing a "for you" attitude toward those for whom the confession was a deficient exposition of God's "for me."[19]

The tidy logician might not always rejoice in the poet's art, but frequently the latter is able to communicate a feeling which brings one closer to the truth than all the "ergos" of the systematicians and the Scriptural citations of the exegetes. It is perhaps true that Selnecker communicated more of the "for me" through his hymns than he did through his theological treatises. The two, of course, ought not be separated, but the distinction expresses an insight into the "art" of the communication of the Gospel. When in Selnecker's own life he sensed a discordant rupture resulting from the *rabies theologorum*, he would get the "for me" and the "for you" together again by expressing himself in verse. And even though he resented taking up a particularly hard-to-live-with neighbor's cross,[20] he spent most of his ministry suffering the exiles which resulted from his attempt to embody a "for you" attitude toward both sides of two contending parties.[21] However, toward the end of his life, after having been forced by his enemies to leave his position three times, he seemed to lose his ability to see any good on the other side. Since he experienced no "for you" from them, he responded in kind and lumped his Christian opponents with unbelieving Jews and Turks.[22] The "for me" of the Formula of Concord began to harden into a dogma which he could confess with his lips but only with difficulty with a life transformed into a continuing "for you."

But ultimately the unvarnished deathbed confession of all four formulators to the "for me" of the Gospel serves as the most eloquent expression of genuine Gospel, a Gospel which intends to transform its recipient into a "for you" type of person but a Gospel which nevertheless remains "for me" in spite of my lagging "for-youness." This was the concord proclaimed by the Formula of Concord and its formulators, and that this message should have also brought discord is understandable in the light of its source in Jesus Christ. His life climaxed in the discord of the cross. Should His followers expect anything less?

Yet we would be naive to think that all discord was born of such faithful discipleship. As we have seen, the formulators of the Formula of Concord were every bit as human as any of us—and accordingly subject to the same weaknesses, the same root-sin, the same tendency to obey vested interests rather than a "for me" Lord. This comes to expression not so much in the written form of the Formula as it does in the manner in which it was implemented. Jesus preferred crucifixion to forcing His "peace formula" on His opponents. The formulators, except for Chytraeus and perhaps Chemnitz during his final illness, were more prepared to crucify than be crucified.[23] Jesus had fellowship with those who sought Him in humble faith (Luke 15:2). He "excommunicated" the proud and haughty (Matt. 15:7-14). But He promoted the "exile" of no one and even forbade His disciples to engage in such "pyrotechnics" (Luke 9:51-56).

In spite of the temptation facing the formulators to become court theologians and to serve as sanctifiers of the status quo, there are examples of prophetic judgment being pronounced also upon a prince. We find this boldness more in Chemnitz and Selnecker[24] than in Andreae and Chytraeus. Of the latter two Andreae was inclined to hitch his star to that of the prince,[25] whereas Chytraeus under ducal pressure preferred to sacrifice his academic integrity rather than risk his academic career altogether.[26] It is certainly gross error to look upon the Formula of Concord as nothing but "political theology," but it would be almost as erroneous to believe that its formulators (and accordingly also its formulations) were free from the subtle influences of the political milieu in which the Formula "happened."[27]

Our investigation has shown how each of the four chief formulators of the Formula of Concord contributed something which, when it is omitted from our reading of the Formula, tends to distort its meaning so that it becomes a source of discord rather than concord. Jakob Andreae contributed a relentless determination not to give up in the struggle for unity until God granted His blessing (Gen. 32:26; Eph. 4:3). Martin Chemnitz lent scholarly and pastoral gifts and a "bishop's" oversight to the entire project (1 Tim. 3:1-7; Eph. 4:11-13). David Chytraeus, as a pious lay theologian, made available his wealth of historical and Biblical knowledge and reminds us of the necessity of maintaining a Christian and humanist disposition (1 Cor. 13; Eph. 4:2). Nikolaus Selnecker offered a scholarly and poetic sensitivity alerting us to his own weakness and that of others (Ps. 51; Eph. 4:14-15). Thus a genuine Formula of Concord is a gift of the Spirit of Jesus Christ to His "body, joined and knit together by every joint with which it is supplied, when each part is working properly" (Eph. 4:16).

FOOTNOTES

Introduction

1. Schlink, pp. xv—xvii; 20 f.

2. Ibid., pp. 9 f.

3. See below, pp. 39, 41.

4. At this point it should be made clear that the present study does not pretend to be a general historical introduction to the Formula of Concord. Such "histories" are already easily accessible to the English-speaking public and ought to be consulted for more detailed information on the general historical setting leading to the Formula. Our purpose here is rather to provide this public with a greater amount of material on those four men most directly responsible for the framing of the Formula of Concord and to pay more attention than is commonly done in Lutheran confessional circles in America and elsewhere to the inevitable but often unnoticed close relationship between the "everlasting Gospel" and the thoroughly historical circumstances coming to expression in the formulated confessions of that Gospel, in this case specifically the Formula of Concord.

5. Roland H. Bainton, *Christendom*, I (New York: Harper and Row, 1966), 96, reminds us, for instance, of the social conflicts lying behind the Donatist controversy, which on the surface appeared to be of a purely theological nature. That rising nationalism and its demand for a means of expressing self-identity lay as one of the motives behind many of the theological criticisms of the papacy already before the Reformation is common knowledge.

6. *The Book of Concord*, ed. Tappert, p. 468, par. 19.

7. Ibid., p. 477, par 17.

8. Guersching, pp. 140 f.

9. A strong caution against overemphasizing the effect of the Peace of Augsburg on subsequent theological development is issued by Peter F. Barton, *Um Luthers Erbe: Studien und Texte zur Spaetreformation. Tilemann Heshusius, 1527—1559* (Witten: Luther-Verlag, 1972), pp. 8 f. He considers the Consensus Tigurinus of 1549 to have had greater significance. It is clear, however, that the events of 1549 and 1555 are interrelated. Barton's excellent study ought nevertheless be consulted for his important suggestion regarding a distinction between "late Reformation" (1549—ca. 1590) and "early Orthodoxy" (pp. 9 f.).

10. Gensichen, pp. 197 f.

11. Contemporary historians of the Reformation differ in their usage. Most remain neutral by employing neither modifier; however, Hajo Holborn almost consistently speaks of the Religious Peace of Augsburg. His use of the word "Religious" not only follows German idiom but is evidently intended to be ironic. See his *A History of Modern Germany: The Reformation* (New York: Alfred A. Knopf, 1967), pp. 243—46.

Jakob Andreae—The Supplanter?

1. Bente, p. 247.

2. Johannsen, p. 406; Fittbogen, pp. 46, 78; Guersching, pp. 138, 140 f., 148; Mueller-Streisand, pp. 230, 246, 266. The most kindly disposed of Andreae's biographers is Pressel, *Die fuenf Jahre . . .*, p. 264.

3. Sasse, pp. 153, 187, 217.

4. Hermelink, pp. 19 f.

5. Maurer, II, 473 f.

6. Joh. Val. Andreae, *Fama Andreana reflorescens* (Strassburg, 1630). It is of interest to note that a complete edition of J. Andreae's works was planned before the end of the 16th century but did not materialize. There is evidence of an attempt to suppress publication of "everything without discrimination" and without the imprimatur of the then highly orthodox theological faculty at the University of Tuebingen. See Mueller-Streisand, pp. 227, 360; Hermelink, pp. 122 f.

7. Guersching, pp. 123 f. Jakob was the eldest of four children. His father died early and his mother remarried.

8. Mueller-Streisand, p. 251. Schnepf was driven from his chair at Tuebingen for opposing the Interim in 1548. From that moment on he moved toward the position of the Gnesio-Lutherans and helped to organize the University of Jena. Cf. Hermelink, pp. 62 f., 74—82, 89—91.

9. Mueller-Streisand, p. 247; Pressel, *David Chytraeus*, p. 5. Luther earned his master's at age 21 in Erfurt and Melanchthon at age 16 in Tuebingen, though he had supposedly been denied it at Heidelberg a year earlier only because of his youth. Maurer, I, 28 f., however, cautions against giving too much weight to such promotion examinations, claiming they had little educational value and reflected more the student's background than his academic achievement.

10. Andreae had ambitions to study at Wittenberg with Luther and Melanchthon, but his promise to the duke never to leave the University of Tuebingen prevented him from doing so. Never did he forget the debt of gratitude he owed the duke for the aid in financing his studies. This financial dependency on the "state" may have contributed to his development as a "state church" theologian. See Mueller-Streisand, pp. 246 f. It seems as though Andreae never did make the personal acquaintance of Luther. Melanchthon he met once, in 1557 (ibid., p. 312).

11. The 25-year-old "doctor" held a disputation on theses treating the doctrine of justification in reference to the questions raised by Osiander (Mueller-Streisand, p. 254).

12. For this and the following see Mueller-Streisand, pp. 256—66.

13. The followers of Flacius desired a church in which discipline was regulated by the clergy, whereas Luther accorded the local parish a larger role. See Mueller-Streisand, pp. 230, 260.

14. For this distinction between a suprahistorical apocalyptic figure and a historical prophetic figure I am indebted to B. A. Gerrish's essay entitled "John Calvin on Luther," *Interpreters of Luther*, ed. J. Pelikan (Philadelphia: Fortress Press, 1968), pp. 87 f. See also below, fn. 78 and text.

15. Mueller-Streisand reports the incident (it occurred in 1553) on the basis of Andreae's own published description of the same (1560); ibid., pp. 267—71.

16. Ibid., p. 267. See below, pp. 41—45.

17. See above, p. 23.

18. Both Guersching, pp. 127, 131, 133, 153, and Mueller-Streisand, pp. 231, 271, 275 f., underscore this point.

19. Mueller-Streisand, pp. 273 f., 319.

20. Ibid., p. 319.

21. Cf. 1 Cor. 3:1-3; Heb. 5:11-14; also 1 Tim. 6:3-5; 2 Tim. 2:14. Here the point seems to be a dynamic growth into maturity, not a static Christian caste system.

22. Muelier-Streisand, pp. 276—78.

23. For this and the following see Bente, pp. 181 f., 238 f.; Gerrish, pp. 82—85; Mueller-Streisand, pp. 282—314.

24. Though Brenz wrote an approving preface, Amsdorf felt differently. He wrote (see Mueller-Streisand, p. 287): "Some say they condemn Zwinglianism, but the preface which Brenz wrote for the book by Dr. Jakob of Goeppingen indicates something quite different. For here they would make a concord between Blessed Luther and Zwingli, if it pleases the gods—which is utterly impossible. Who ever heard that one could make a concord between contradictory viewpoints?" On the other hand, Calvin also is unconvinced. He writes (ibid., p. 300) that though he appreciates Andreae's consistently even-tempered attitude towards him, even in the midst of the attacks directed against him by Westphal and the Saxons, nevertheless it hurts him to learn that they differ more than he had thought. He hopes that their dissension would not lead to hostility and hatred, which though hidden the Lord would also finally expose.

25. Mueller-Streisand, p. 302.

26. Ibid., pp. 326 f.

27. Ibid., pp. 327—32, 349.

28. Ibid., p. 332; Hermelink, p. 91.

29. In the Formula of Concord the "ubiquity" of Christ is taught either in Brenz's form of "ubivolopresence" or Chemnitz's form of "multivolopresence." See Sasse, p. 341; Schlink, p. 189.—It was during this period of time that Melanchthon supposedly said of Andreae: "God grant that no one encourage this Swabian, otherwise he will stir up a great deal of trouble throughout the German states." In 1581 students at Wittenberg composed a drinking song based on the Lord's Prayer containing words like:

> Blasted Jakob, who art in Swabian ubiquity . . .
> Thy devilish will be done neither in Wittenberg nor in Leipzig.

See Guersching, pp. 134, 144. In 1560 Melanchthon had referred to the confession of the Stuttgart Synod as "Hechingense Latinum," implying that it was similar to a local dialect and therefore could not be a teaching of the universal church (Bente, p. 179; Guersching, p. 140; Mueller-Streisand, p. 332). But Rogness argues that Melanchthon was not opposed to the ubiquity of the total Christ but only to a manner of speaking which dealt with the two natures of Christ as abstractions rather than always considering them unified in the Person of Christ. See Rogness, pp. 72 f., 130.

30. Mueller-Streisand, p. 332.

31. Hermelink, pp. 122 f., refers to the Wuerttemberg of this generation as developing into the "Lutheran Spain" and to Tuebingen as the future "center of orthodoxy."

32. Mueller-Streisand, pp. 350 ff. In spite of his frequent absences from home on special assignment, he became the author of more than 200 books and brochures.

33. See above, pp. 23 f.

34. Strigel maintained that "the will is passive insofar as God alone works all good, but active insofar as it must be present in its conversion, must consent, and not resist, but accept." See Bente, p. 135.

35. Mueller-Streisand, pp. 352—58. That Andreae was sensitive to the relationship between the doctrines of justification and the Lord's Supper is suggested by Mueller-Streisand, pp. 282, 291.

36. Ibid., p. 359.

37. Ibid., p. 362.

38. Ibid., pp. 362 f.

39. Tappert, pp. 589 f. See also Sasse's analysis, pp. 308 f., of the "Wittenberg Concord" of 1536, an expression of the minimum requirement for a possible agreement between Lutherans and "Zwinglians."

40. Mueller-Streisand, pp. 363 ff.; Bente, pp. 199 ff.

41. Johannsen, p. 383.

42. Mueller-Streisand, pp. 366 f.; Guersching, pp. 142 f.; Johannsen, pp. 356, 362 f.

43. Mueller-Streisand, pp. 367—71.

44. See above, pp. 25, 27 f.

45. Mueller-Streisand, pp. 334—36.

46. Johannsen, p. 345.

47. Ibid., pp. 346 ff. Andreae attempted to win the Gnesio-Lutherans for a document without condemnations by reminding them that Luther was content with such in the formulation of the "Wittenberg Concord" of 1536. See also Bente, p. 243.

48. A detailed account of the development leading from Andreae's "Five Articles" to his *Six Christian Sermons* is given by Robert Kolb, "Six Christian Sermons on the Way to Lutheran Unity," *CTM*, XLIV (1973), 261—74.

49. Johannsen, pp. 346, 354 f.

50. See above, pp. 32 f.

51. This does not at all imply that colloquies were not held between representatives of opposing viewpoints (as any history student knows), but they were held in an atmosphere in which participants tended to think of themselves only as teachers rather than also as learners, i.e., each was confident of the absolute correctness of his formulations (or at least of the possibility in principle of making such formulations), whereas today we are more sensitive to the relativities attaching to all historically conditioned formulations (or at least to the tremendous difficulty of arriving at generally understood formulations). Nor had Andreae himself arrived at this point, but perhaps he more than others of his generation sensed the need for something other than an inflexible standing by a formulation once made.

52. See above, p. 35.

53. Johannsen, pp. 357—61; Bente, p. 243; Kolb, pp. 265 f. Bente cites the Wittenberg theologians as having been dishonest in this case, whereas Johannsen interprets the evidence so that Andreae becomes the dishonest culprit. Guersching, p. 144, reports how Andreae and the news of his slanted minutes of the meeting at Zerbst were

received in Wittenberg. Each time he cited Luther in his defense he was heckled by protesting students, whereas at each mention of Melanchthon's name these same students ostentatiously raised their barrets in a salute to their hero.

54. See H.-W. Gensichen, pp. 155—57.

55. Mueller-Streisand, p. 277.

56. Guersching, pp. 144 f., lists some of the colorful labels given Andreae at this time. In Jena he was called "the dunderhead who wanted to presume on God's prerogatives," since he placed his hope in his own skill at diplomacy. No more complimentary was the title "medicine man" given him at Wittenberg, since he tried to cure everything by palliatives except the Wuerttembergian ubiquity dogma. Meanwhile his fellow Wuerttembergians were accusing him of botching his assignment through his impatience and of having failed to follow strictly the instructions of Brenz, who died just a few days before Andreae's arrival home from Zerbst and Wittenberg.

57. Johannsen, pp. 364, 368 f.; Guersching, p. 146. It seems that the appearance of the anonymously published *Exegesis perspicua* (1574) and the support this Calvinistically oriented document received from his theologians opened the eyes of August to the problem in his own "house." For the intrigue and mystery surrounding these proceedings see Bente, esp. pp. 189 f., 245.

58. Kolb, p. 269, points out how Andreae cleverly omitted these personal condemnations from the text proper of his sermons but entered specific names of false teachers in the margin alongside their views as these appeared in the printed edition of his *Sermons*.

59. Johannsen, pp. 364 f.

60. According to Pressel, *Die fuenf Jahre . . .*, p. 6, this was simply Chemnitz' polite way of suggesting to Andreae that merely to have his name appended to a work aroused the suspicions of many and it would be better if the *concordia* did not go out under his name.

61. Montgomery (quoting Fritschel), pp. 20—22.

62. Johannsen, pp. 367 f.; Guersching, pp. 147 f. Johannsen interprets Andreae's motives as having been self-seeking, whereas Guersching sees him as being ambitious only for the sake of unity itself.

63. See above, p. 37.

64. Pressel, *Die fuenf Jahre . . .*, p. 8, suggests that behind this move lay the political and religious rivalry between the two Saxon houses. See also Guersching, pp. 140 f.

65. Johannsen, p. 369.

66. At the same time August asked Duke Ludwig of Wuerttemberg to release Andreae to him for the carrying out of this concordistic activity, which as it happened stretched itself out between the years 1576 and 1580. During this time Andreae's wife and two sons lived with him, first in Leipzig and then in Wittenberg. See Pressel, *Die fuenf Jahre . . .*, pp. 40, 42.

67. Bente, p. 246. But Heshusius remained bitterly opposed to the person of Andreae, whom he still considered guilty of offense for having tried to harmonize the doctrine of Luther and Calvin and for having supported Strigel at Weimar. See above, pp. 30 f., and Pressel, *Die fuenf Jahre . . .*, pp. 44 f.

68. Montgomery, pp. 21 f.

69. In the Tappert Edition the Epitome covers 30 pages whereas the Solid Declaration is 136 pages in length.

70. Johannsen, p. 376. Cf. Tappert, p. 502, par. 6.

71. The prevention of such a synod at this time was tactically speaking a wise move. But it was advisable also on theological grounds, as is made clear in a projected (but never incorporated) preface to the FC composed by its authors. Here it is argued that a doctrine stands or falls on the authority of God's Word and not on that of a general synod. It is well that doctrine be confessed before a synod and by a synod but its basis always remains independent of a synod—God's Word. For this reason acknowledgment of doctrine on the basis of this Word should precede synodical activity. See Pressel, *Zwei Actenstuecke . . .*, pp. 711, 741 f.

72. See above, pp. 39 f.

73. See below, pp. 82 f.

74. Johannsen, p. 385.

75. Cf. the editor's footnote in the Tappert Edition, p. 11, fn. 5.

76. See below, pp. 53 f., where the distinction between exclusion and expulsion is discussed in terms of the distinction between *excommunicatio minor* and *excommunicatio major*.

77. Bente, p. 248.

78. Another, though quite different, expression of this phenomenon was that of the revolutionary French Huguenots. See above, pp. 24 f., 29. The notion of perfecting rather than abolishing goes back to St. Thomas. See J. Pelikan, *The Riddle of Roman Catholicism* (Nashville: Abingdon Press, 1959), pp. 147 f. It is necessary to distinguish between culture per se and the sinful state in which we find it. The prophetic Word seeks to abolish the sin while it also seeks to sustain and perfect culture itself.

79. See, e.g., Bente, pp. 249 f. Sasse, pp. 331 f.

80. Guersching, pp. 127, 131, 137, 146, 151, 153, 156.

81. Bente, pp. 247—49.

82. The Greek root of the word "martyr" means to witness, to confess.

83. The complicated history of this Preface is mentioned in only one sentence by Bente (p. 247), whereas Johannsen devotes no less than five pages to it (pp. 398—402). The footnotes to the Preface in the Tappert Edition, pp. 3—14, give some idea of what was at stake. For full documentation see also the Goettingen Edition, pp. xli—xlii, 739—62. To neglect this history is to neglect seeing the "expulsion" tactic for what it was—the use of church discipline for the purpose of achieving political-ecclesiastical rather than patently evangelical ends.

84. Owen Chadwick, *The Reformation* (Baltimore: Penguin Books, 1964), pp. 146 f.

85. Johannsen, p. 406.

86. Pressel, *Die fuenf Jahre . . .*, pp. 239—49, reproduces this document in full. A translation is given in our Appendix IV.

87. Johannsen, pp. 404—15.

88. Otto Schmoller, *Zwanzig Predigten von Jakob Andreae aus den Jahren 1557, 1559 und 1560* (Guetersloh: Bertelsmann, 1890), pp. 16 f.

89. See the article by Arthur C. Piepkorn under "Andreae, Jakob" in *The Encyclopedia of the Lutheran Church*, ed. Julius Bodensieck.

90. Guersching, p. 156.

Martin Chemnitz—The Confessor?

1. Cf. "An Autobiography of Martin Kemnitz," in *Theological Quarterly*, III (October 1899), 474 (translation there by A. L. Graebner). Chemnitz had an eye for historical detail and, as we shall yet note, was not altogether averse to consulting the stars as one of his sources.

2. Ibid., p. 473. "Treuenbrietzen" means "Faithful Brietzen."

3. Ibid., pp. 473, 475.

4. Ibid., pp. 474 f.

5. Ibid., p. 475. The Luther whom Chemnitz heard at this time was the Luther of the Smalcald Articles.

6. Ibid., pp. 475 f.

7. Ibid., p. 476.

8. Ibid., p. 479.

9. Ibid., p. 479.

10. In his hand Chemnitz carried a valuable letter of recommendation written by Melanchthon and addressed to his son-in-law Sabinus. This letter and eight others by Melanchthon having to do with Chemnitz are printed with introductory notes and comments prepared by Friedrich Koldewey in *Zeitschrift fuer die historische Theologie*, XLII (1872), 3—23.

11. *Autobiography*, pp. 480 f. Piepkorn, p. 9, fn. 9, agrees with John Warwick Montgomery that the 20th century is inclined to take what may be too jaundiced a view of the interest of men like Melanchthon and Chemnitz in astrology. Their Scriptural justification for such astrological studies was Rom. 8:28, which, of course, does not teach a fatalistic, deistic determinism but a living faith that God's "got the whole world in His hands" and that this God is "for us" in Christ Jesus.

12. Ibid., p. 481.

13. Ibid., p. 480.

14. Ibid., p. 481.

15. Ibid., p. 482.

16. This event has actually been called the second Martin's "tower experience." Cf. Klug, p. 127.

17. Chemnitz, *Autobiography*, p. 483.

18. Bente, p. 153, writes: ". . . this personal element added largely to the animosity and violence of the controversy that was soon to follow, and during which the professors in Koenigsberg are said to have carried firearms into their academic sessions."

19. Ibid., pp. 152—54.

20. Chemnitz, *Autobiography*, p. 483.

21. Piepkorn, p. 7.

22. Chemnitz, *Autobiography*, p. 483.

23. Ibid., p. 483.

24. Ibid., p. 484.

25. Ibid., p. 485.

26. Cf. Koldewey, pp. 7—9. Melanchthon seemed to sense that Chemnitz' allegiance was being given to Chemnitz' friend and Melanchthon's opponent, Moerlin. In a postscript to a letter dated March 24, 1556, Melanchthon wrote Chemnitz: "I beg you meanwhile to write us lest you allow the memory of my friendship to be extinguished in your soul" (pp. 7, 13 f.). Chemnitz hastened to answer and discussed a "neutral" subject—the comet which had recently appeared and about which Melanchthon had inquired (p. 21, fn. 19).

27. Koldewey, p. 8, reports how Chemnitz met Melanchthon only once more in a face-to-face situation—the embarrassing circumstance of being one of a number of delegates from north Germany who at the instance of Moerlin were sent to Melanchthon to obtain an explanation (in effect a recantation) relative to the adiaphoristic and synergistic controversies. At the time Melanchthon shouted: "You have come to murder me!" It was probably Chemnitz' kindly disposition toward his former teacher which influenced his colleagues to be satisfied with a promise from Melanchthon that he would make concessions. It is possible that Melanchthon and Chemnitz confronted each other personally once more at the ill-fated Colloquy at Worms in 1557. See above, p. 17.

28. Ibid., pp. 7 f., 10 f., 15. Here Koldewey reproduces letters Melanchthon wrote to Chemnitz on the occasion of his marriage and at the death of his firstborn, Martin, at 11 months.

29. Herman Hachfeld, p. 143.

30. Ibid., p. 79.

31. Ibid., pp. 14, 82, 85.

32. Pressel, *Martin Chemnitz*, p. 39.

33. Hachfeld, pp. 17 f.; Bente, pp. 238 f. Brenz and Andreae were among those whose acquaintance Chemnitz made.

34. Pressel, *Martin Chemnitz*, pp. 15—20, esp. 19—20.

35. Robert Preus, pp. 48 f. However, even an admirer like Hachfeld, p. 42, is critical of what appears to him to be an abstract, metaphysical God concept that serves as the point of departure in Chemnitz' dogmatics.

36. Pressel, *Martin Chemnitz*, pp. 25 f., 40.

37. Hachfeld, pp. 18 f.

38. Pressel, *Martin Chemnitz*, pp. 26 f.

39. Ibid., pp. 27 f.

40. Hachfeld, pp. 20 f. Cf. above, p. 18.

41. Hachfeld, ibid.

42. E. g., ibid., pp. 34 f.

43. The best review of this controversy in the English language is to be found in Piepkorn, op. cit. Consult the extensive bibliography cited there.

44. See above, p. 17.

45. Piepkorn, p. 13. Piepkorn here cites Chemnitz as he hits hard at the Jesuit assertion that "nonecclesiastics ought not to ask if the things proposed to them are right or otherwise, but ought humbly kiss the hinder parts of the chapter in canon law which begins *Si Papa*."

46. Piepkorn, p. 29, defends Chemnitz' appeal to the witness of the fathers as more than

fleshly arguments. Chemnitz' Scriptural-Gospel sling is not without its history, and he is honestly concerned with standing in the continuity of the church committed to it. One of Piepkorn's sources, Reinhard Mumm, pp. 62—64, judges otherwise and argues that whereas Chemnitz, like his teacher Melanchthon, assuaged his doubts by resorting to a dogmatic-historical construction, Luther more quickly turned in simple trust to God. A critical attitude toward Mumm's analysis is taken by Klug, pp. 116, 138—40. He points out, p. 131, that the words of Vincent of Lerins in 434 ("Now in the Catholic Church itself we take the greatest care to hold that which has been believed everywhere, always, and by all") are characteristically adapted by Chemnitz to read ". . . hold that which has been received consistently from Scripture, always, everywhere, and by all believers."

47. The *Examen* was originally published in four successive parts, viz., Parts One and Two, 1566; Parts Three and Four, 1573. Each part was dedicated to a Lutheran prince or his son, a practice frequently followed by theologians at this time to "buy insurance" for their theology from secular (though Christian) sources. Cf. Piepkorn, p. 19.

48. Mumm, p. 77.

49. Hachfeld, pp. 52 f.

50. Pressel, *Martin Chemnitz*, p. 34.

51. Ibid., pp. 34—38.

52. Ibid., pp. 38 f.

53. Klug, p. 133, cites C. G. H. Lentz as arguing that Chemnitz' volume on the Person of Christ, *De duabus naturis in Christo*, was completed in handwritten form already in 1567, even though it was not published until 1570. If so, it is no wonder that Chemnitz had no difficulty conducting his doctoral disputation in 1568.

54. Hachfeld, pp. 55 f.; Klug, p. 230.

55. Hachfeld, pp. 13, 56—58; Pressel, *Martin Chemnitz*, pp. 47 ff. Eduard Bodemann in his study, pp. 1—92, portrays Julius as a superpatriotic prince, committed both to his people and to the Hapsburg emperor (Maximilian II). Bodemann registers disappointment with Julius only to the degree that he appeared politically shortsighted and theologically ultraconservative, extraordinarily willing to accede to the "narrowly Lutheran" opinion of his theological advisers, such as Chemnitz and Andreae (ibid., pp. 19, 35 f.; also above, pp. 34—36).

56. Pressel, pp. 48—53; Hachfeld, pp. 57—59.

57. Pressel, ibid., p. 51. The *Corpus doctrinae Julium* consisted of: (1) Chemnitz' 12 articles dealing with the controverted doctrines; (2) the three ecumenical creeds; (3) the Augsburg Confession; (4) the Apology; (5) the Smalcald Articles; (6 & 7) Luther's two catechisms; (8) the treatise by Urbanus Rhegius (1481—1541, Lutheran reformer in Lueneburg) entitled: "How one should with care and without offense speak about the chief articles of Christian doctrine"; (9) and Chemnitz' "well-substantiated statement of the chief (11) articles of Christian doctrine, how in each case one may and ought to speak of them with modesty on the basis of God's Word" (added at the request of Duke Julius in 1576). The liturgical and ecclesiastical ordinances were not original with Chemnitz but were rather borrowed for the most part from the Lueneburg Order (1564) and that by John Brenz and Duke Christoph of Wuerttemberg (1559).

58. See above, pp. 37—45.

59. Hachfeld, pp. 63—66.

60. Hachfeld, p. 74.

61. See above, p. 43, and Hachfeld, pp. 73—78. Among the first professors were outspokenly orthodox Lutherans such as Tim. Kirchner, T. Heshusius, D. Hoffmann, and B. Sattler.

62. See above, pp. 34 f.

63. Pressel, *Martin Chemnitz*, p. 57; Hachfeld, p. 105.

64. Hachfeld, p. 106.

65. Ibid., p. 107.

66. Ibid., pp. 107—109.

67. Cf. Tappert, *The Book of Concord*, p. 590, par. 119. Also Wilhelm C. Linss, "Biblical Interpretation in the Formula of Concord," in *The Symposium on Seventeenth Century Lutheranism, Selected Papers*, I (St. Louis, 1962), 131: "Among about fifteen different versions and commentaries consulted, there were only two which supported the translation of the *Formula of Concord*—Luther and Bengel. All the others, including the *King James Version, Revised Standard Version*, Zahn, Kittel (Traub), revised Luther (1956), advocate the translation rejected by the *Formula of Concord*. The Greek itself is ambiguous."

68. Hachfeld, p. 112; also the translation by J. A. O. Preus of Chemnitz' *The Two Natures in Christ* (St. Louis: Concordia Publishing House, 1971), pp. 10 f.

69. Hachfeld, p. 113.

70. See above, pp. 35, 37, 39.

71. Hachfeld, p. 115.

72. See above, pp. 37—45.

73. Hachfeld, pp. 118 f. Some months later, at Tangermuende on March 10, 1578, after a further revision of the FC had been considered, Chemnitz let it be known that the insertion of a single word would prompt him to blot out his subscription (ibid., p. 120).

74. See above, pp. 61 f.

75. Bodemann, pp. 33—41. For Chemnitz' advice to Julius in this matter see our Appendix II.

76. See above, p. 43; Piepkorn, p. 10; Tappert, *The Book of Concord*, p. 612, pars. 9 and 10.

77. Similar reasons were probably at work when the Brunswick City Council with the support of the ministerium (which would include Chemnitz) protested the August 1578 mandate of Duke Julius affording Jews the permission to live within the city. Cf. Hachfeld, p. 127. We have already above, pp. 24 f., related another account which dramatically reveals the moral limitations and the rootedness in history of our Lutheran forefathers.

78. Hachfeld, pp. 123—32; Bodemann, pp. 41 f.; Johannsen, pp. 401—404.

79. Piepkorn, p. 10; Hachfeld, p. 131.

80. At this meeting Chemnitz and Andreae also completed the *Catalogus testimoniorum*, which appears as an appendix to the Formula of Concord and was intended to document that the confession stands solidly in the tradition of the ancient church in its doctrine of the Person of Christ.

81. Chemnitz, for example, wrote a letter to Andreae in which he frankly compared the latter's recent behavior over against Duke Julius and himself as being "like the cat

which licks from the front and scratches from the back." Cf. Pressel, *Martin Chemnitz*, p. 69; Johannsen, p. 403.

82. Johannsen, pp. 402—404; Hachfeld, pp. 131 f.

83. Noth, pp. vii, ix; R. Preus, pp. 48 f.; Klug, pp. 136 f.

84. Pressel, *Martin Chemnitz*, p. 69.

85. Hachfeld, pp. 129, 134—36. See the important monograph on Heshusius by Barton, esp. p. 232.

86. See above, pp. 60 f.

87. Hachfeld, pp. 136—39.

88. Mumm, pp. 36—40.

89. Hachfeld, p. 42.

90. Noth, pp. 55—57; Mumm, pp. 56 f., 65—76; Elert, pp. 45, 54 f.; above, p. 49. It is interesting to note, however, that although Mumm, p. 57, argues that Chemnitz' struggles were more intellectual than they were struggles with Satan, as were Luther's, Noth, p. xi, nevertheless cites the following title: *Andaechtige Gebete wider die Teuffel in den armen besessenen Leuten/etc. gemacht von D. Joach. Moerlino, und D. Mart. Chemnitio, zusammen getragen von Melch. Neukirchen/Helmstaedt 1596.* Chemnitz also argued for the retention of the exorcism in the baptismal rite in the following way (cf. Pressel, *Martin Chemnitz*, p. 52): "Inasmuch as we in the churches of this city retain the exorcism, the preachers ought from time to time in their sermons remind the people that the same ought not to be understood thus, as though the child were rescued from the power of the devil through the exorcism and not through Baptism; rather, the exorcism is to be understood as a reminder of the great need and wretchedness in which the little child is caught because of his sins, for which very reason he needs Baptism and that which Baptism works in him."

That Satan was not demythologized between the publication of Luther's catechisms and the FC is at least in part due to the fact that one of the final editors of the FC, Andrew Musculus (see above, p. 12) was closely associated with the development of a literary genre known as "Teufelliteratur." Cf. Gruemmer, pp. 27—61.

91. Cf. above, pp. 122 f., fn. 46. Among the evidence considered ought to be the comparative views of Luther and Chemnitz on such questions as the nature of the Biblical canon and of the ministerial office and the form of the words of absolution. Superficially, at least, Chemnitz seems to place a different emphasis on the formal aspects of these matters (even to the point of retaining the title of "priest") than does Luther. Cf. Mumm, pp. 48, 59, 62, 70.

92. See above, pp. 26—28, 30—32.

93. Hachfeld, p. 142; also see above, pp. 50, 53 f., 57 f., 63 f.

94. Pressel, *Martin Chemnitz*, p. 71.

95. Ibid., pp. 39, 70; Hachfeld, p. 139.

David Chytraeus—Alter Philippus?

1. The name "Kochhafe" means "cooking pot," as does its Grecization "Chytraeus." David had nine brothers and sisters, of whom one brother, Nathan, became a philologist and poet and fellow faculty member with David at the University of

Rostock, while two other brothers bacame pastors. David was later deeply grieved by the conversion of Nathan to Calvinism.

2. Pressel, *David Chytraeus*, p. 3.

3. See above, p. 22.

4. Pressel, *David Chytraeus*, p. 4.

5. See above, pp. 21 f.

6. Montgomery, p. 11.

7. Pressel, David Chytraeus, p. 5. After testing Chytraeus' ability to translate a passage in Thucydides from Greek into Latin, Melanchthon is reputed to have said: "You are without doubt a 'master,' and you will be as precious to me as a son."

8. Cf. *Luther's Works: Lectures on Genesis*, Vols. 7 and 8 (St. Louis: Concordia Publishing House, 1965 and 1966).

9. Pressel, *David Chytraeus*, p. 6.

10. Ibid., p. 6; above, p. 48.

11. On one occasion Chytraeus wrote Duke Joh. Albrecht an enthusiastic account of the significance and value of astrology. He called his attention to the "celestial globe" of Til. Heshusius and indicated how astronomy refreshes man's exhausted spirit by lifting it to the heavenly fatherland. This is the case especially if men then "in genuine invocation call upon the Son of God, the director of the stars and the guardian of pious rulers, and in firm faith yield themselves in the midst of every peril to His very own protection and defense. . . . So don't let your eyes be glued to the ground but most diligently pursue this God-pleasing study. In every age kings have loved astrology and busied themselves with it, and so an appreciative world subsequently honored the eternal stars with their names. . . . Next to Scripture it is astrology which leads to the knowledge of God" (Klatt, p. 9).

12. Pressel, *David Chytraeus*, pp. 6—7.

13. Ibid., p. 9.

14. Ibid., p. 10.

15. Klatt, p. 7. Klatt emphasizes the important place which the study and teaching of history had among the encyclopedic interests of Chytraeus. His versatility is simply evidenced by the fact that whereas Klatt characterizes him chiefly as a historian, Montgomery, p. 8, insists that he was by interest and temperament an exegete. Meanwhile Robert Preus reminds us that he "reveals a definite dogmatic leaning," p. 104.

16. Klatt, pp. 18—21. Chytraeus suffered from headaches, kidney pains, and gout. He frequently was confined to his bed for weeks and even months at a time. Within an 18-year span (1562—1580) he recorded the deaths of four daughters, three sons, and his first wife. At the time of their death his children ranged from age five months to 15 years. During this period of sorrow he composed his work: *De morte et vita aeterna*, the first Lutheran monograph on eschatology. Klatt calls our attention to the significant fact that Chytraeus had an aversion to the taking of medications. He felt that illnesses were best treated according to the rule of Celsus through patience, rest, and abstinence (p. 20). One wonders how Chytraeus felt about the propriety of seeking healing from the Lord. Would this also inevitably have to be considered an attempt to escape the cross?

17. Pressel, *David Chytraeus*, p. 15. The above excerpt is taken from an address which Chytraeus held on the 75th anniversary of Luther's birth and entitled: *De studia*

theologiae. . . . . It emphasizes the character of theology as being "practice" rather than mere theory, as consisting in action rather than in mere knowledge. Cf. Robert Preus, pp. 104—107.

18. Montgomery, pp. 7, 13 f., argues against this evaluation by Georg Loesche. It is true, of course, that Chytraeus' commentaries are not "scientific" in the modern sense, but that is not altogether a liability. Cf. Montgomery, pp. 28 f.

19. See the translation by Montgomery, op. cit.

20. Pressel, *David Chytraeus*, pp. 10 f.

21. Ibid., p. 12. Also Barton, pp. 124—27. Here Chytraeus is quoted as referring to Heshusius as "the outstanding jewel and protection of this church and university." In 1561 Chytraeus wrote a letter to Heshusius in which he made very clear the influence the latter had had in drawing him firmly out of the Philippist and into the Lutheran camp.

22. Klatt, pp. 7 f.

23. Ibid., pp. 129—42. Klatt, p. 10, cites Chytraeus as saying: "He who does not know how to endure slander, envy, abuse, and insults does not know the first thing about how to live."—A fine characterization of Dukes Johann Albrecht and Ulrich and of the ecclesio-political scene in Rostock, with the intense controversy between the pro-ducal "preacher-party" and the anti-ducal "city-council-party," is given in Barton, pp. 121—31, 142—57. The entire narrative reflects how Chytraeus' strength lay in the friends he chose to support rather than in his own independence and convictions.

24. According to Klatt, p. 10, Chytraeus shared with Melanchthon the latter's feeling about the *rabies theologorum.*

25. See above, p. 17.

26. Roland Bainton, *The Reformation of the Sixteenth Century* (Boston: Beacon Press, 1952), pp. 197 f., 236 ff. Also Robert Bolt, *A Man for All Seasons* (New York: Vintage Books, 1960), pp. 86—95.

27. Klatt, pp. 16 f., has the following to say: "The question as to how Chytraeus inwardly stood in relation to the later Melanchthon will undoubtedly have to remain open, since he never clearly expressed himself on the matter. Love and devotion for his teacher most likely prevented him from critically evaluating his writings; secondly, he probably also feared that taking such a decisive position would only serve to intensify the theological controversy; and finally he did not consider it absolutely necessary to commit himself irrevocably on issues which were really debatable." Although Klatt recognizes the force of these arguments, he concludes that one must still hold Chytraeus guilty of a certain *dissimulatio.* It seems, however, that Melanchthon found the "silence" of Chytraeus more eloquent than Klatt is willing to admit. Pressel reports how Chytraeus once said to Duke Johann Albrecht: "As long as Philip and Flacius are alive no unity will be able to be effected between the rival parties." This was reported to Melanchthon in another version, viz.: "No unity can be hoped for until Philip has been eliminated." Melanchthon began to fear for his life, and even after the matter was clarified and the issue clearly defined as being theological, not biological, he declared: "I would rather be murdered in public than choked into silence by such decrees" (Pressel, *David Chytraeus*, pp. 19 f.).

28. See the article by Arthur C. Piepkorn under "Chytraeus, David" in *The Encyclopedia of the Lutheran Church.*

29. See above, p. 18; Bente, pp. 242 f.; Montgomery, pp. 19 f. Chytraeus, together with the

Saxon theologians Moerlin and Stoessel, warned against the acceptance of editions of the Augsburg Confession other than the *invariata*. Earlier both Chytraeus and Selnecker spoke mildly of the edition of 1540 and thought to find in it "no variation of the essential doctrine."

30. Pressel, *David Chytraeus*, p. 22.

31. Ibid., p. 23.

32. Ibid., pp. 15 f., 26 ff. A Lutheran hermeneutic is given us here, which reads as follows: "In matters dealing with the faith, such as anything that touches upon the present religious controversy and the disunity in doctrine and worship, the one, eternal, changeless norm shall be the Word of God as revealed in the churches' holy, divine Scripture. . . . Accordingly it is necessary diligently to compare the sayings of the prophets and apostles, especially as they appear in the Hebrew and Greek original and in their proper contexts, and thus arrive at a meaning that is in harmony with the sum of Christian doctrine and agrees with the totality of Holy Scripture. Thereupon the commentaries and testimonies of approved teachers, particularly Luther, may also be used and considered. Insofar as they echo the harmonious sum of divine doctrine they establish all the more firmly the intention of and the adjudication by the God-fearing critic. But in any case our faith and confession are grounded not upon man's own writings, but upon the holy, divine Word," p. 27.

33. Ibid., p. 23.

34. See above, p. 17.

35. First choice of the emperor was N. Selnecker, but he declined. The call was then accepted by Joachim Camerarius, but he met with hostility because of his close association with Melanchthon (see above, p. 70). Chytraeus was then the third choice. See Pressel, *David Chytraeus*, p. 29.

36. See above, pp. 32 f., 36; Pressel, ibid., pp. 28 f.; Klatt, pp. 17 f., 136 f.

37. See above, p. 59.

38. For an explication of the conservative/ecumenical character of these church orders and their widespread influence see my dissertation *Die Brandenburg-Nuernbergische Kirchenordnung von 1533 und ihre Auswirkung* (Erlangen, 1964).

39. Klatt, pp. 17 f. Bodemann, pp. 12—20, emphasizes the role of Lazarus von Schwendi in seeking a reunification of the churches for the sake of saving the empire and his disappointment with the "narrowly" Lutheran perspective of his friend Duke Julius of Brunswick.

40. Pressel, *David Chytraeus*, p. 30.

41. Ibid., pp. 30 f.

42. Ibid., p. 31.

43. Ibid., pp. 31 f.

44. See above, p. 56.

45. Pressel, *David Chytraeus*, pp. 33 f.

46. Ibid., pp. 35 f.

47. Ibid., pp. 29, 36. Above, p. 77.

48. See above, pp. 34—36.

49. Johannsen, pp. 354 f.; Pressel, *David Chytraeus*, p. 37.

50. See above, pp. 37 f.

51. See above, pp. 37—41.

52. See above, p. 77.

53. See Appendix III A.

54. Pressel, *David Chytraeus*, p. 38. Although Chytraeus indicated that he personally had not yet come to any conviction on theological issues such as that of the ubiquity of the human nature of Christ and the "communication of attributes," he felt that of all theologians Chemnitz had written most wisely on the subject (ibid., p. 37). An English translation of several extended quotations from Chytraeus' work on the Augsburg Confession is given in Schmauk and Benze, esp. pp. 291, 305.

55. Montgomery, pp. 20—23. Montgomery here refers to the research (only partially published) of J. Fritschel, who prepared an account of the genetic development of the individual articles of the Formula of Concord. Fritschel specified exactly the not insignificant contributions by Chytraeus to the Formula as a whole.

56. See above, pp. 38—41.

57. See above, pp. 39 f.; Montgomery, p. 22.

58. See above, pp. 40 f.

59. Johannsen, p. 381.

60. See above, pp. 40 f.

61. He wrote in a letter: "I prefer the 'Torgau Book' to the 'Bergic' in many respects. The former was altered without my participation by the 'triumvirate' in March. Later also three others of us [Chytraeus, Musculus, and Koerner] were 'as a matter of form' summoned to participate, but everything had already been decided upon ahead of time. Nevertheless I cannot, nor do I wish to, retract what I have once subscribed" (Johannsen, p. 381).

62. Ibid., p. 381.

63. Klatt, p. 17.

64. Pressel, *David Chytraeus*, p. 42. According to Pressel, p. 40, the Rostock faculty had earlier also complained that the FC contradicted the AC on the doctrine of the Lord's Supper and transubstantiation, that it misrepresented the Sacramentarians, that it used the term *damnamus* rather than the milder *reiicimus* and *improbamus* and that Melanchthon's name and authority received no thankful recognition. In his article on the FC in *The Encyclopedia of the Lutheran Church* Wilhelm Maurer seems to share some of the concerns of the Rostock faculty, for he writes (II, 872): "The sentence in the Apology that 'justification is regeneration' (IV, 78, 117, 313), which without question takes justification in the effective sense, is reinterpreted in the sense of imputation; and justification and sanctification are viewed as two temporally distinguishable successive events (SD, pars. 40—43). The repeated appeals to AC, Apology, and Luther's second series of lectures on Galatians are not quite legitimate."

65. See above, pp. 74 f.

66. Pressel, *David Chytraeus*, p. 43.

67. See above, p. 60.

68. Pressel, David Chytraeus, pp. 44 f.

69. Klatt, passim, esp. pp. 60—64, 119—24. Thus Chytraeus practiced a brand of "situation ethics."

70. Ibid., pp. 53—60, 150—89.

71. The precise year of Chytraeus' birth is uncertain, the sources varying from as early as 1529 to as late as 1531. See Montgomery, pp. 10 f.; Klatt, pp. 4 f., 20 f.

72. Klatt, p. 12.

73. Robert Preus, pp. 100—103. He writes: "It is difficult to see why Chytraeus saw any need of these evidences, especially the external ones, for the truth of Christianity."

74. Pressel, *David Chytraeus*, p. 46.

75. Ibid.

76. Ibid. Pressel concludes: "However, throughout all the Protestant churches there tolled death's lament—the last representative of the most fertile century in world history was laid to rest in the first year of a new epoch; the faithful disciple of Luther and Melanchthon was gathered to his fathers."

Nikolaus Selnecker—The Weather Vane?

1. Article on Selnecker by D. Wagenmann in RE, 2nd ed., 14 (1884), 76—88; revised by F. Dibelius in RE, 3rd ed., 18 (1906), 184—91.

2. In 1582 Selnecker published a report on Veit Dietrich's (d. 1549) orthodoxy, defending him against the claims of the Sacramentarians. See Bernhard Klaus, pp. 308 f.

3. King Ferdinand when visiting Nuernberg once invited the young Selnecker to play the Magnificat for him at Vespers, at which time he intended to "kidnap" him for his own service as a court musician. Selnecker's father, however, got wind of the plan and kept his son in hiding. See Koch, p. 160.

4. See above, p. 70.

5. (Wagenmann) Dibelius, p. 185.

6. Ibid.

7. Ibid.

8. Greiser (d. 1591) had been a student of Schnepf and Brenz and followed a strict Lutheran line. He helped Selnecker to become acquainted with the writings and teachings of these two theologians from southern Germany. See Wagenmann, p. 77.

9. (Wagenmann) Dibelius, p. 185. Margaretha bore him 15 children, of whom 10 died in infancy. Those who matured (three sons and two daughters) all entered or married into the ministry or teaching profession (ibid., p. 189).

10. Wagenmann, p. 78.

11. Polack, pp. 428, 578 f.

12. F. Dibelius, "Zur Geschichte und Charakteristik Nikolaus Selneckers," *Beitraege zur saechsischen Kirchengeschichte*, IV (1888), p. 9.

13. Ibid., pp. 11 f.

14. Polack, p. 211.

15. Dibelius, pp. 13 f.

16. Ibid., p. 15.

17. Ibid., pp. 15—17.

18. Polack, p. 211.

19. (Wagenmann) Dibelius, p. 186.

20. Ibid.

21. See above, pp. 29—31.

22. Koch, p. 162.

23. Strigel had been professor at Jena from 1548 to 1562, where he carried on a running battle with the Flacians until he succumbed to their pressure and left. See above, pp. 30 f.

24. See above, p. 17.

25. Wagenmann, pp. 78 f.; see above, pp. 34—36; 128, fn. 35.

26. See above, p. 36.

27. (Wagenmann) Dibelius, p. 187.

28. Wagenmann, p. 80; above, pp. 123 f., footnotes 53 and 68.

29. See above, p. 62.

30. Wagenmann, p. 80. For an account of some of the early tension between Selnecker and Chemnitz, see Hachfeld, pp. 105—14.

31. (Wagenmann) Dibelius, p. 187.

32. Georgius Le Smannus, *Nuetzlicher Geschichts-Calender* (Leipzig: Christoph Huelsen, 1698), pp. 37 ff.

33. Wagenmann, p. 81; see above, pp. 60 f.

34. Ibid.

35. (Wagenmann) Dibelius, p. 187. Dibelius points out how the bowdlerized version of Selnecker's hymn line "Halt mich bei *reiner* Lehr" loses precisely that which was characteristic of Selnecker, who actually prayed "Halt mich bei *deiner* Lehr."

36. "Lions and wolves." Wagenmann, p. 81. For an indication of the confidence Duke Julius had learned to place in Selnecker see Bodemann, pp. 22 f., where we hear of the duke soliciting from Selnecker an opinion on the advisability of following Queen Elizabeth's suggestion of forming an all-Protestant league against the Catholics. Selnecker's advice to the duke in 1572 agreed in principle with that given by Chemnitz in 1577. See above, p. 63.

37. See above, pp. 60 f.

38. Polack, p. 239. For an interpretation of this hymn in the light of the historical events surrounding its composition see Dibelius, pp. 4, 18—20.

39. See above, pp. 37—39.

40. Wagenmann, p. 81, Dente, pp. 189—92.

41. See above, pp. 39 f.; Bente, pp. 244 f.

42. Pressel, *Die fuenf Jahre. . .*, pp. 26—30; Bente, p. 246.

43. See above, p. 39.

44. Gruemmer, p. 87. In March of 1580 Musculus wrote to Elector Johann Georg of Brandenburg: "Experience will finally demonstrate, as can already be seen from the accompanying, what happens when such important matters are dealt with in such haste. The dear church of old willingly spent more time even when dealing with less important matters, and even then the yield was hardly bountiful; all of which makes me wish, the longer and the more I consider these things, that I had never been dragged into

the deal. The Son of God marvelously rules and preserves His church, and He will not permit Himself to be ruled by men, as the outcome of all councils and synods testifies and demonstrates."

45. Pressel, *Die fuenf Jahre . . . ,* pp. 31—33.

46. Wagenmann, p. 82; Pressel, *Die fuenf Jahre. . .,* pp. 34 f., 40, 44.

47. See above, pp. 40 f.; Pressel, *Die fuenf Jahre . . .,* pp. 46 f.

48. See above, pp. 96 f.

49. See above, pp. 40 f.

50. See above, pp. 91—93.

51. Pressel, *Die fuenf Jahre. . .,* pp. 238 f. A translation of Selnecker's "report" is given in Appendix IV.

52. Ibid., pp. 207—64. The case is extremely complicated and difficult to unravel, the evidence being as elusive of definitive interpretation as the testimony emerging out of the notorious "Watergate hearings" of the early 1970s. Pressel's discovery in the Gotha Library of a vast holding of original documents surrounding the case has made available evidence similar to the "White House tapes" in the Watergate affair, but these have by no means betrayed all the secrets locked in the hearts of the personalities involved.

53. See above, pp. 98 f.

54. See above, pp. 64, 82—84.

55. Pressel, *Die fuenf Jahre. . .,* p. 257.

56. Ibid., p. 261.

57. See above, pp. 64 f.

58. For the intriguing story of this plot see Bente, p. 190.

59. (Wagenmann) Dibelius, p. 188.

60. When Lutheranism was once again established under Christian II (1591), Crell was imprisoned and 10 years later (1601) tried by the imperial court at Prague, found guilty as "an enemy of peace and a disturber of the public quiet," and beheaded "not on account of his religion, but on account of his manifold perfidy" (Bente, p. 192).

61. See above, p. 98.

62. (Wagenmann) Dibelius, p. 190. In addition to compositions by other reformers this hymnal contains 130 of Selnecker's own hymns. On the title page he wrote:

> Luther leads us all in song,
> Tenors out God's Word so strong.
> Him we follow twitter-fashion,
> Knowing God will have compassion.

Only a few of the melodies are original with Selnecker, but his two "Passions" (Matthew and John) as well as his setting of the "Threni" (Lamentations of Jeremiah) have been accorded enduring recognition in the history of church music. It is no accident that J. S. Bach and Selnecker lie buried in the same church. See the article by Walter E. Buszin under "Selnecker, Nikolaus" in *The Encyclopedia of the Lutheran Church.*

63. Koch, p. 165. Notice the play on words when Selnecker refers to Calvin's doctrine as "calcified" (reproducing the German "kahlen Lehren"). Selnecker's son and son-in-law were also banned by the Crell government.

64. Wagenmann, pp. 83 f. In verse he said: "Oh, keep us in Thy Word, we pray; The guile and rage of Zwinglians stay!"

65. Koch, pp. 166 f.

66. Ibid., p. 167.

67. Ibid. Also Buszin, op cit., III, 2155.

68. Ibid.

69. Ibid.

70. On Dec. 21, 1580, Andreae wrote Elector August: ". . . for this reason, then, Your Grace need not be concerned that I might become involved in a public, offensive feud with Selnecker, for his inconstancy and lack of commitment are more generally known than is pleasing to me and for the sake of our common task I have frequently had to suppress this knowledge in the minds of people in places high and low" (Pressel, *Die fuenf Jahre. . .*, p. 253).

71. See above, pp. 98 f.

72. Winkler, p. 99.

73. Ibid., pp. 94 f.

74. Ibid., p. 100.

75. Ibid., p. 101.

76. Polack, pp. 211, 230 f., 239, 428, 577 f.

77. (Wagenmann) Dibelius, p. 190.

78. Ibid., p. 191.

79. Ibid.

80. See above, pp. 101—03.

81. Polack, p. 230.

The Formulators—Of Concord or Discord?

1. Schmauk and Benze, p. 681.

2. See above, pp. 35, 61, 81, 96—98.

3. See above, pp. 39 f.

4. See above, pp. 43 f., 64.

5. See above, pp. 44, 101—03.

6. See above, pp. 82 f.

7. See above, p. 97.

8. See above, pp. 36, 38, 42 f., 64.

9. See above, pp. 64, 83 f., 100 f.

10. See above, pp. 50 f., 70 f., 90 f.

11. See above, pp. 42 f., 57 f., 85 f., 101—03.

12. Barton, pp. 10, 13 f.

13. See above, pp. 24 f.

14. See above, pp. 41—44.

15. See above, pp. 53 f., 57 f.

16. See above, pp. 63 f.

17. See above, pp. 64 f.

18. See above, pp. 74 f.

19. See above, pp. 83—85.

20. See above, pp. 101—03.

21. See above, pp. 93—96, 103 f.

22. See above, p. 104.

23. Though Luther in theory carefully distinguished the "greater excommunication" (civil penalties; what I call "expulsion") from the "lesser excommunication" (spiritual penalties; what I call "exclusion") and maintained that ministers of the church are not concerned with the former, in practice, because he was dealing with a territorial church and in a cultural situation which could not tolerate more than one church in a given territory, this distinction often became blurred and the church's image when dealing with dissenters often appeared more Caesarlike than Christlike. Cf. SA III/IX (Tappert, p. 314). See above, pp. 53 f.; 120, fn. 76.

24. See above, pp. 63 f., 93—95.

25. See above, pp. 21—23, 27, 43 f.

26. See above, pp. 74, 85 f.

27. See above, pp. 15 f.

Appendix

I. Preface to Andreae's Sermon on Matthew 24
Dealing with Controverted Articles of Faith[1]

Dr. Jakob Andreae hereby wishes all God-fearing Christians of high and low estate in Thuringia and Franconia grace and peace in Christ Jesus.

There is no doubt that many God-fearing Christians have been grossly offended by the multitudinous changes which have occurred in the churches and schools of these territories within the past few years. There is also no Christian who doubts that these occurred at great risk but that God had His reasons for permitting them to occur. Thereby God not only punished thanklessness over against His Word, but He also desired to test His chosen ones, as silver and gold is tested through fire, whether they might hold to their simple Christian faith and not permit themselves to be blown hither and yon by every wind of doctrine.

Yet God is so good that He permits nothing evil to happen unless He also knows how to use it for good. This is observable in the case of mankind, for in this instance God revealed His love for the children of men in that His Son became a man and the Father, wonder of wonders, poured out an entire heart full of mercy for us poor sinners. Apart from His knowing how to turn evil into good this would not have occurred and we would have remained ignorant of this goodness. Now we see something similar happening in connection with this present chaos.

For had such turmoil not occurred and the preaching of the Gospel had been consistently promoted without any division and offensive schism, people would have taken it for granted and would not have recognized it as a special expression of God's grace. However, now that they have seen how contradictory doctrines have been introduced into the churches and schools one after another and how even the teachers who beforehand had been united are condemning and anathematizing each other in a fashion miserable to behold, God-fearing Christians are learning properly to recognize the pure teaching of God's Word together with true Christian unity as the highest gift God can bestow upon His children on earth. For what a miserable picture churches and schools present when teachers and preachers are divided in their own midst, their congregations split, the people embittered against one another. This we would much prefer to forget than most painfully to repeat. How much more should we prefer to look to God's gracious and fatherly will, for He desires by means of such offensive schisms to make His Word all the more precious and dear to us. The case is similar to that of a man who has lost a precious jewel which was especially dear to him; should he once again find it, he seeks to preserve and protect it with greater diligence than he would had he never lost it.

Therefore after having come so close to losing God's Word as a result of so many different schisms and yet there having been awakened by the special providence of the Almighty and the urging of the Holy Spirit the preeminent, illustrious prince and ruler, our lord Augustus, Duke of Saxony, Grand Marshal and Elector of the Holy Roman Empire, Landgrave in Thuringia, Margrave in Meissen and Burgrave in Magdeburg, etc., our most gracious lord, let us hope that, by His Electoral Grace's gracious decree and encouragement and as a result of the pure, unadulterated Word of God and of our simple holy Catechism, the desired Christian unity in all disputed articles will be attained in the churches and schools of this land, the pulpits cleansed, and public doctrine again be restored to the original state to which Dr. Luther, now sainted, had brought it before his Christian death.

Accordingly, teachers and students but particularly God-fearing housefathers should encourage, remind, and admonish each other and their children—seeing they all but lost God's Word but, praise God, have it again restored—that they receive it henceforth with the greatest thanksgiving, maintain and preserve it all the more dear and precious, and with all diligence see to it that they not once again and for the last time lose it completely and finally.

This grace of God ought to be appreciated all the more since the aforementioned turmoil of faith and Christian teaching occurred at a time when people were still living who could testify to the pure doctrine as well as to the manifold, earnest warnings against the schisms threatening to follow upon his death which they heard from the blessed lips of Dr. Luther. All of these people gave public testimony to their heartfelt joy when the newly arrived-at concord was signed by all superintendents, pastors, and other ministers of our churches and schools, and they thanked God Almighty from the bottom of their hearts that they should have lived to see the hour in which by the special grace of God the doctrine lately brought to light by Dr. Luther should again have broken forth after having in various and many ways been beclouded and suppressed. Similarly such a public testimony coming from the older clergymen in these territories, those who had reached 70 and even 80 years, was received with great thanksgiving to God by hundreds, yea thousands, of people as the arrived-at concord was signed unanimously and joyfully by all superintendents, pastors, and ministers of churches and schools.

Since that is the case, we should not only diligently thank the Almighty for such grace but also as Christians gladly and willingly forgive and not maliciously remember regarding one another that which during such turmoil occurred of an unrighteous nature and which none other than the enemy of all mankind and especially of Christendom perpetrated. Furthermore we should diligently pray that God would be pleased to maintain intact this precious treasure of His pure unadulterated Word and Christian unity.

It was at the persistent and earnest request of many Christians that I allowed myself to be moved to publish the sermon I gave on Nov. 24 at Weimar. In that sermon I proclaimed to the Christian congregation this Gospel regarding the Christain unity of the ministers of the church. If you as a Christian should wish to know its content in a most brief and summary fashion, you should realize that it is nothing else than your simple Christian Catechism. For in spite of the length of time that we quarreled about these questions, it finally turned out that your simple, holy, Christian Catechism is divine and indubitable truth. Whoever teaches contrary to it should know that he has fallen short of divine truth.

Accordingly, if anyone wishes to be saved and to be preserved against all error, he should hold to his Catechism with simple faith and not permit himself to be driven from it even by a hairsbreadth.

May the Almighty God and Father of our Lord Jesus Christ grant that to all of us through the Holy Spirit. Amen.

II. Chemnitz' Advice to Duke Julius Regarding the Protestant Alliance Proposed by Queen Elizabeth[2]

Nov. 27, 1577

. . . As for the invitation you received from England, the lettering almost proves who is behind it. And when I consider the line of argumentation used therein, I am inclined to think that it had its origin not in England but in Germany. I thank our good and faithful God, who so clearly rules the heart of Your Grace, that Your Grace has not been misled or provoked into rash action but rather is taking Christian counsel as to how such measures are to be avoided. Since Your Grace has graciously desired that I express my concerns relative to the chief points of the English invitation, I have in humble obedience brought myself briefly to spell out the same. First of all, Your Grace will know both at the beginning and at the end of the letter how winsomely and politely to express what pertains to the offer of an ongoing correspondence and friendship, namely, that Your Grace had sought the same from Her Majesty by means of her service as godparent and that it was your further intention, etc. And since the invitation deals in some points with doctrine and therefore with questions of conscience, but in other points with political friendship and negotiations, Your Grace will wish to respond differently to each point, reflecting thereby the difference between matters of conscience and matters dealing with politics. Accordingly the points dealing with doctrine are the following:

1. The question of why there should be negotiations in Germany regarding a new religious confession, whereas one would do well to stick with the old and not call into question that which once electors and princes worked out and subscribed relative to these religious issues.

2. The fact that all this is occurring at an inauspicious time, seeing that so many matters and changes are in the offing.—Your Grace can respond squarely to both points, since first of all it has never been the intention to produce or to accept a new religious confession and to depart from the old, and secondly, this task was not just embarked upon this year, but Your Grace from the very beginning of your office (as can be found in *A Tract on the Reform of the Churches* that since the time of the Interim many things have been introduced by a number of theologians which do not measure up to the old Augsburg Confession and to Luther's teaching) has out of a sense of Christian responsibility been concerned both as to how Your Grace's churches and schools might be reformed in accordance with the original teaching of the Augsburg Confession as practiced at the time of Luther and as to how what arose as novel and contrary thereto might be censured and hindered, as did then occur in the Church Order commissioned by Your Grace.

Since this Church Order and example were approved by the most prominent of the new churches, Your Grace further considered whether ways and means might not be found whereby with God's grace the churches of the Reformation in Germany might be drawn together out of their more recently experienced divisions and again restored to a basic, durable, and God-pleasing agreement in classic Lutheran teaching as originally expressed in that first Confession as it was subscribed by the electors and princes at that time. Four years ago Your Grace initially undertook this plan in conjunction with churches of Lower Saxony and Swabia, which for their part through frequent correspondence conferred with you and sought your leadership. Thereupon an initial draft was prepared, drawing upon the Augsburg Confession, the Apology, the Smalcald Articles, the Catechisms and other approved writings of Luther which agreed with the norm of the Word of God, and this was subjected to the critique of the various churches for improvement. When once other electors and princes of the empire reviewed it and sensed the propriety of continuing this work (which had been begun for good reasons and had been constructed on a firm foundation), Your Grace was approached two years ago by the other electors and princes for the task of "selling" the described Formula. Now after long and mature consideration this resulted in the approval of the Formula by nearly all the churches in the empire. And the remaining churches are engaged in responsible discussions

138

concerning it. Thus the Formula was composed for good reasons, namely, that Your Grace as well as other electors, princes, and estates might finally determine to walk in the footsteps of the original protesting electors and princes. Accordingly this is nothing novel nor is it something just now coming into being.

3. Therewith also Point 3 can be considered answered, namely, that this task was originated and supported by subtle undertakings of the Papists.

4. The supposition that only one point was especially being disputed, namely, that concerning the Supper of the Lord.—In this regard Your Grace on the basis of God's Word maintained that it was not a peripheral but a central article, that it touched upon the testament and the majesty of the Lord Christ and how faithful children and servants might properly conduct themselves over against the testament and good name of their Parent and Lord, etc.

5. The fact that the estates of the empire could thereby be moved to split from one another.—Your Grace is aware of no reputable estate which publicly allied itself with the doctrine of the Sacramentarians. That a few estates are still disputing about the Formula is not due to disagreement on the article regarding the Supper, and actually the matter is by God's grace on the way to being adjudicated, etc.

6. The question raised by the Formula's condemnation of other churches in many lands and this without a hearing; thus also the fact that Germans assume for themselves the jurisdiction over other churches in other lands, etc. That one should also consult other foreign churches when desiring to undertake such a task.—This work was begun and undertaken not in an attempt to arrogate to oneself the jurisdiction over other kingdoms but to clarify how the protesting princes in the empire from the very inception of the Reformation, for themselves and without appeal to other nations, in accordance with their own conscience on the basis of the Word of God, drew up their church orders in reference both to doctrine and ecclesiastical ceremonies. Also as to how they rejected and condemned false doctrine in their churches, and this without regard to whether there were such as promoted this doctrine in other nations or even in Germany itself. Accordingly the protesting electors, princes, and estates undertook this work for the German churches in order once again to establish the same by God's grace in the united confession of classic Lutheran doctrine and to turn aside foreign opinions such as were contrary to such classic Lutheran doctrine. Since then the Formula was not sent out to arbitrate over those in other nations but was sent only to the Reformation churches of Germany, Your Grace maintains that the churches abroad have no basis for harboring ill will against the princes of

Germany as the invitation implies. The national churches of other lands were accordingly not condemned, seeing that the majority of these had not been instructed other than in the doctrine of the Sacramentarians; but false doctrine must on the command of Christ be reproved and the laity must be warned regarding it. Therefore one dare not praise such teachers as instruct the people falsely and thereby confirm them, together with the others, in false doctrine. It is as clear as day what troublesome things are being written by the Calvinists against our church's doctrine concerning the Lord's Supper.

7. Regarding the fact that in the Formula there are found novel and untraditional expressions and paradoxes, etc.—In this case the problem is only apparent, since the expressions are drawn from the Augsburg Confession, the Apology, the Smalcald Articles, the Catechisms, and other writings of Luther. As a matter of fact many of these difficult expressions are avoided in the Formula, and so Her Majesty the queen ought not seem to evaluate the Formula so harshly on the basis of secondhand reports.

8. The charge made in the invitation that this work was provoked by the greed and ambition of a few theologians.—This can be convincingly refuted since the work was directed by the electors and princes themselves with the advice of the theologians of all the churches to the end that the divisions threatening these churches might be powerfully thwarted and that provision might be made against such threats in the future.

9. This point can be answered by saying that is was assumed that the result of the Marburg Colloquy in 1529 was public knowledge. At that time the theologians did not wish to recognize the Zwinglians as confessional brothers, nor did the electors and princes wish to acknowledge them as confessional allies even though the arguments produced at that time were the same as those put forward in the present invitation. Accordingly it is nothing new when we confess in the article on the Lord's Supper: "They disapprove of those who teach otherwise." The fact, however, that in the years 1557 and 1561 the zealous example of our predecessors was not followed has become the very reason why the protesting estates had to undertake this present work.

10. The charge, among other things, that words of condemnation are employed, etc.—This can be answered simply by indicating that the words "reject, disapprove, condemn" as used in the Formula are taken from the Augsburg Confession.

These are roughly the points in the English invitation which deal with doctrine and to which I have at the behest of Your Grace given my simple response. This would have to be fleshed out and subjected to proper protocol. Other matters dealing with political concerns as, for instance, the machinations of the Papists, likewise the fact that the protesting estates of the realm ought not let themselves be divided but should remain allied against the common enemy, the Pope, these Your Grace will know well how to explain and irrefutably answer.

III, A. Preface to Chytraeus' History of the Augsburg Confession[3]

To the illustrious, gracious, noblest, and best, to the rulers and the royal and noble subjects of the Dukedom of Steiermark, a land worthy of praise. My gracious and magnanimous lords.

As certain and as indubitably true as it is that there is an only, eternal, Almighty God, who in this beautiful, glorious creation of heaven and earth and of all creatures has revealed His divine wisdom, goodness, and power and has clearly manifested and presented Himself to all angels and men to be praised by them, so certain and indubitably true is it also that this one and only eternal God—this dependable, faithful, and incomparable Savior-God—has out of His immeasurable goodness and mercy through His divine Word proclaimed to mankind His divine essence and will and our Savior Jesus Christ and the eternal blessedness of mankind. Subsequently He had this recorded in writing in the Holy Bible and confirmed it with glorious and reliable evidences and miracles. What is there taught is the only sure basis of our entire Christian faith and eternal salvation. It is the eternal rule and norm according to which all our thoughts regarding the proper knowledge and worship of God and regarding all service and obedience rendered God throughout our entire life are to be established and judged. For this purpose therefore God has now created all people and redeemed them through His Son that they might be God's image and dwelling place, wherein the eternal Creator and our Redeemer and Savior, Jesus Christ, might be properly recognized, implored, and adored. For this reason in particular has God established congregations in kingdoms and cities, namely, that they be God's dwelling place and temple wherein might shine the true knowledge and worship of God and our Savior Jesus Christ and all God-pleasing virtues. Also that our precious youth might be instructed and educated by faithful and diligent teachers and schoolmasters, that as a result of the fear of God and profitable teaching they honor God and thereupon carry out God-pleasing service both for the sake of their own welfare and that of others. And that in public assemblies, in churches and schools everywhere, God be worshiped, praised, and adored.

Now granted that Your Grace's praiseworthy and precious fatherland, the Dukedom of Steiermark, has been adorned and blessed more than many other lands with many great and glorious gifts by God, yet Your Grace as a Christian and highly informed ruler recognizes that people live together in principalities, cities, and homes and daily have intercourse with each other particularly for this reason, namely, that one properly instruct and teach the other in the things of God and our Savior Jesus Christ and that by one's doctrine and confession regarding God and by the example of other virtues one might lead and bring other people to the proper knowledge of Christ and true divine blessedness. Also that in government, courts, homes, and businesses righteous behavior might be mutually exercised in order that we realize that God is righteous, faithful, generous, and merciful and that we should be conformed to Him by such virtues; and that in public assemblies, in churches and schools, all with united voice call upon God, thank, praise, and glorify Him. As it is written in the Psalm not only regarding the single city of Jerusalem but in general of all Christian cities and principalities:

> Jerusalem, built as a city which is bound firmly together,
> to which the tribes go up, the tribes of the Lord,
> as was decreed for Israel,
> to give thanks to the name of the Lord. [Ps. 122:3-4]

Accordingly, Your Grace will also consider this to be the most necessary and best jewel of all and the highest badge of honor for your praiseworthy and precious fatherland, that therein is taught, maintained, and spread the one, eternal, true doctrine regarding GOD and our Savior Jesus Christ and our eternal blessedness. Also that rulers and subjects alike come together in public worship assemblies in order to minister to our Lord God and to preach and proclaim His Word and merciful deeds. And finally that the true understanding and worship of God, together with such other necessary teaching and skills as are required and useful in the conduct of both the holy ministry and secular government, be transmitted and maintained in churches and schools.

Seeing then that Your Grace condescended to call and use me as a humble and dedicated servant for the sake of counseling with some of the churches and schools in Your Grace's territory and seeing that you were pleased to show me such gracious favor for the sake of my diligence and faithfulness in spite of my failings and also beyond this to display toward me during the entire time that I spent in Steiermark every gracious and friendly expression of goodwill and generously to have honored me and those of my house, I am accordingly from the bottom of my heart thankful to Your Grace for these generous benefits and as a humble expression of my appreciation wish to ascribe and dedicate to Your Grace (in addition to the other reasons also because Your Grace, along with many other Christian kings, princes, and estates, has committed yourself to it as to a standard or brief summary and digest of the pure and faithful doctrine of the Gospel) this *History of the Augsburg Confession*, in which I describe how the same took its beginning, was originally composed, was submitted to Emperor Charles V at the

Diet of Augsburg in the year 1530, and then was defended and vindicated by an extensive Apology. Included is also an account of other discussions and events dealing with the religious questions as they were raised at this selfsame diet. This I have done at the special behest of several prominent and outstanding citizens. Some diligently requested this as a result of their own feelings, but then also particularly at the urging of Your Grace's and Steiermark's chief minister, Mr. Matthew Amman, whose faithfulness and diligence in all matters pertaining to the preservation and promotion of the glory of God and your territory's reputation, honor, good name, prosperity, and success is very well and already for many years known to Your Grace. It is our hope, therefore, that Your Grace will find this our candid reflection and undertaking, which has accordingly occurred at the good and timely advice of others, not as something unpleasant or offensive but rather as something honorable and perhaps also to be commended to our descendents.

As to the composition of this entire work itself, I have faithfully compiled from the reliable and for the most part already published documents and writings of those who were firsthand witnesses and representatives of the events herein described, first of all the material written in Latin (a copy of which I also submitted to others). Each writing I put in the chronological order in which it appeared whether before or during the diet. Then those writings which were originally in Latin I translated or had others translate into German. I particularly paid attention to avoid including any writing which was unofficial or spurious or would contribute to anyone's harm or loss of reputation.

I also diligently sought advice and counsel regarding this entire work from a variety of God-fearing, sensible, and learned men and particularly from the pastor of the churches in Wittenberg and superintendent of the Electorate of Saxony, Dr. Caspar Eberhard. They provided much in terms of suggestions, documents, correspondence, and other writings and faithfully brought to my attention numerous items, encouraging me to share this with others by seeing the work through the press. It is hoped that it will prove useful to the many Christians committed to the Augsburg Confession and to other goodhearted people, not only as a necessary source of information regarding many extremely important matters but also as a comfort and source of strength for faith subjected to danger and persecution as a result of the confession of the Gospel and as a testimony to the divine providence and wondrous protection and preservation afforded the churches which have committed themselves to the Augsburg Confession.

However, insofar as this report is hereby for the first time being published in this authorized version and anyone could easily expand it by adding the Apology or items dealing with the more secular aspects such as the procession of the emperor and princes into Augsburg, his crowning at Bologna, the details surrounding the celebration of the Mass with subsequent procession, etc., likewise any number of private writings and correspondence such as arose between scholars in connection with the diet and which were indiscriminately copied and distributed, nevertheless I hereby appeal that others might let this work remain unchanged and unimproved in spite of what might appear to be inadequate in it.

Seeing then that I have endeavored to recount only the religious aspects of this diet, I have intentionally omitted the political song and dance and other matters which were carefully recorded by Master George Spalatin and otherwise were of particular interest to the curiosity mongers. The fact that I did not wish to rush into print such correspondence and private writings that have not yet been publicly authorized but of which I have a goodly amount in my possession is the result of seeking and following the advice of informed, learned, and peace-loving theologians as well as other people. For in this material there is much that would not serve the good name not only of scholars but also of highly reputable people and princely houses and for that reason is better not divulged but buried. However, these matters might perhaps be reported at some other time.

And now I implore the eternal and merciful God, who has called Your Grace to the true understanding and confession of true Christian doctrine as it is briefly, pointedly, and correctly gathered out of God's Word and set down in the articles of the Augsburg Confession, that He might preserve, increase, and strengthen His kingdom as He has established it in Your Grace's heart and in the environs of Steiermark, to the glory of His divine name and to the welfare and salvation of His dear church. Amen. Dated at Rostock in the year 1575 on the 25th day of June, the day on which 45 years earlier the Augsburg Confession was first submitted to Emperor Charles V.

David Chytraeus

III, B. A Testimony by Chytraeus Dealing with the Controversy Regarding the Lord's Supper[4]

Pledged to you are God's grace through His only begotten Son, our Lord and Savior Jesus Christ, and my devoted service and fervent prayer for Your Princely Grace's lengthy and blessed rule.

Gracious Lord.—At Your Princely Grace's gracious command that I obediently report to Your Princely Grace whether before Luther's death there was made between Dr. Luther and John Calvin an agreement whereby they were united in those matters pertaining to the controversy regarding the Lord's Supper, I humbly report as follows. Though I spent several years in Wittenberg before and after Dr. Luther's blessed death, and though I was quite involved in paying attention to what was being published regarding this controversy from its beginning and extending to the time in question, nevertheless I have never been aware of, nor has there ever been brought to my attention, anything regarding such an agreement. As a matter of fact Calvin was first attacked in Germany as a result of the Interim, at which time he allied himself with the theologians at

Zuerich, the disciples and successors of Zwingli. For up to that time, while he was during Luther's lifetime lecturer in theology at Strassburg, he was considered by no one in these parts other than as one who with heart and soul was committed to the Augsburg Confession and to Dr. Luther. The battle against Dr. Luther's and the Saxon Church's doctrine of the Lord's Supper he first undertook publicly against Westphal in the years 1553 and 1554, many years after Luther's death, and from that point carried it on for many years.

Although many years earlier during Luther's lifetime in the year 1536 a "Formula Concordiae" had been established between the Wittenbergers and the theologians of the cities of southern Germany, nevertheless Dr. Luther at that time understood the "Concord" in no other way than that his opponents had left off from their previous opinion and had devoted themselves completely and entirely to his Confession. This is substantiated among other ways also by the document prepared at that time by Elector John Frederick of Saxony for Your Princely Grace's cousin, Duke Henry of Mecklenburg, and dealing with a certain Neiber at Wismar.

In my opinion the two opposing doctrines of Luther and the Calvinists are in this article as far apart as heaven and earth. For Dr. Luther faithfully and consistently taught and shortly before His death repeated that Christ is essentially present in the Sacrament with His body and blood here on earth. The Calvinists on the other hand argue that the essential body and blood of Christ are just as far from the bread and wine in the Sacrament as the highest heaven is distant from the earth. Furthermore that they are only spiritually appropriated by faith, which spans the entire heavens, and that this appropriation is similar to that which occurs in the preached Word and in other Christian devotions, only that in this case there is a simultaneous appropriation of the holy signs.

Accordingly it is difficult to imagine how the two opinions could ever be united so long as each representative faithfully sticks to his opinion, as Dr. Luther without doubt did to his end. This information I obediently once again document at the gracious behest of Your Princely Grace. I thank Your Princely Grace for graciously sending a copy of the Polish treaty. This Your Princely Grace will graciously once again hereby receive. I am at all times ready and duty-bound to render Your Princely Grace humble and obedient service. Dated at Rostock, June 4, 1589.

Your Princely Grace's humble servant,

Dr. David

IV. Selnecker's Diary on Andreae's Behavior[5]

Selnecker. My observations on Dr. J. Andreae during the period between 1576 and the meeting at Jueterbog (Jan. 19, 1579).

April 1576. Originally I sincerely considered him an orthodox teacher and an upright man, particularly when he arrived on April 6, 1576, and discussed with us the question regarding the Sacramentarians and how they were to be resisted. At that time we agreed that he had nothing else in mind than to obtain necessary counsel and support at court from Dr. Vogel, Secretary Jenischen, and Master Lysthenius, as well as to consult Mr. Daniel, Master Petrus Glaeser, and others. That is where matters stood and everything was going along fine until the convention at Torgau at which the theologians of this territory submitted a petition and requested our gracious lord that His Grace might appoint for a period of time to the universities in these territories three men, namely, Dr. Jakob, Dr. Chemnitz, and Chytraeus. At that point Dr. Jakob began to pester me in particular and advised against acquiring Chemnitz and Chytraeus for the following reasons: Chemnitz was supposedly devilish and unfaithful and Chytraeus was nothing but a philosopher and skeptic; they would instigate nothing but trouble, since Chemnitz in particular would want to introduce Heshusius and strict adherents of Flacius into our territory. This kind of talk displeased me, especially when he began to probe my conscience as to whether Chemnitz was a man to be trusted and believed, seeing I knew how matters stood between them when they were in Brunswick and how he himself had written: "Let each one have his own understanding." Thereby he had supposedly attacked the churches of Wuerttemberg and subjected them to suspicion so that the theologians at Wittenberg in their confession had not without reason referred to himself as a "sycophant." Thereupon I urged and admonished him not to say such things, since Chemnitz was a theologian who had accomplished much that was valuable and helpful, as his learned study on the Council of Trent and his book dealing with the Sacramentarians attest. I reminded Dr. Jakob of how I had often designated Chemnitz' booklet "a gem," mentioning this not only at conventions but later to him personally and for his benefit also at public gatherings. However, Dr. Jakob would not permit my point to stand, but indicated that just as he had many serious reservations in regard to the confession of the Saxon churches against our own, so also was he displeased with Chemnitz' book dealing with the communication of attributes. Dr. Chemnitz would have to revise it were he himself to be satisfied with it. Finally he expressed himself thus that he wished to speak with our gracious lord personally and convince him that both Chemnitz and Chytraeus should best be left uninvited. All this immediately set me to thinking and resulted in my becoming suspicious of Dr. Jakob and his ambition, and in several important doctrinal points I found him guilty of new aberration. Nevertheless I didn't want to trust my own feelings but thought: Perhaps the man has other motives and I ought also get to know him better.

During the month of December Einsiedel, Loeser, and Dr. Jakob arrived in Leipzig as official school visitors. The theologians were called upon to answer several questions, which they did. Since these answers, which were in written form, included also reference to the "Torgau Articles" on the question of the Lord's Supper (which we reported were valuable and Christian), Dr. Jakob hastened to point out that the commissioners would be altogether dissatisfied with us, for we would be renewing the suspicion against ourselves if we cited the "Torgau Articles" as authority, and thus the last error would be worse than the first. Accordingly we dropped the reference to the "Torgau Articles." When I asked him what in them was suspect, he answered: "The fact that they do not allow that the Lord's Supper should be based on the ubiquity amounts to a rejection of the ubiquity." This answer caused me a second time to take pause to think; nevertheless I did not yet at this time want to take issue with him.

In March of 1577 at Bergen near Magdeburg, Chemnitz and I frequently and earnestly asked Dr. Jakob that he should not make any independent moves, and though he immediately agreed, he never kept his promise. He inveighed against Chemnitz again and again and adorned him constantly with select adjectives which were altogether foreign and strange to me. Likewise he made mention of a variety of things: (1) of his situation at the court and of his detractors—great _____, windbags, blood-letters, and spies; (2) of several disputations concerning the communication of attributes and the fact that to say "God suffered" is tantamount to saying "the divinity suffered"; that hell, like heaven, is not a place; and should God want to have the devils in heaven, the devil would be for Him a good partner, as a preacher in Swabia is reputed to have correctly said; (3) of his envisioned reformation of the churches and schools in this territory. At that point Chemnitz spoke with me and expressed his opinion that he did not see that this fellow would accomplish anything good. We approached him again and entreated him to take the advice of good people and not to proceed so independently. Dr. Chemnitz also extended him his thanks for promoting him although he had not been called. Thereupon Dr. Jakob offered his continued support in reference to his being called, should he desire this. Nevertheless he also mentioned to him the circumstances at court, how every day he experienced some new opposition, that although at the moment he was in favor, soon he might again be in disfavor. To which Chemnitz replied that he was satisfied with his people at Brunswick and that he knew very well that he, Dr. Jakob, was not serious about calling anyone. However, Dr. Jakob swore stoutly and called God to witness that he would prefer to be home and to grant the honor freely to another. At that time I still had high hopes and did not yet suspect Dr. Jakob of having evil motives but chalked it all up to apparent weakness in the face of his heavy work load; nevertheless I trusted and believed him less than before. In the carriage on the way home he spoke a great deal about the consistories, namely, that they were of no value and ought to be abandoned and that a single ecclesiastical court should be established at the chancery. When I opposed his proposal, he became angry with me, as he himself later confessed and admitted.

During May of 1577 Master Matthesius (with whom, since we live in the same house, I occasionally discussed the fact that he as well as his father-in-law should beware lest Dr. Jakob lead him into some misfortune, for Dr. Jakob was heard to have spoken suspiciously about Master Lysthenius, that my gracious lord should have instructed him through Secretary Jenischen to be on the lookout for some different court preachers) brought to my attention the manner in which Dr. Jakob spoke illusively about me and frequently also about his father-in-law. For instance, he said that: (1) *me carere omni iudicio*, I had no real understanding; (2) I had written against Beza but in a very unclear fashion and had myself not really grasped the proper intention of the ubiquity; (3) someone finally ought to put me in chains; (4) if he had his way, I would be dismissed; (5) I would eventually have to revoke all my books; (6) he intended to convince me that there was a cow whose name was Barthel. Such talk hurt me especially because I would rather anticipate the falling of the heavens than that Dr. Jakob, who to my face constantly refers to me as his lord and dear friend, should unjustly use such language about me behind my back. Therefore it was unavoidable that I should confront him with this, though without disclosing the source of my information. As a result he, together with Dr. Simonius, came to me while in the church of St. Thomas and standing before the crucifix in the chancel called upon Christ to witness that God would punish him in soul and body, now and eternally, and never again be gracious to him, if ever such thoughts should have come to him, not to mention if ever he should have expressed them, but that God should be his witness that he had always thought and said the opposite and that he would do so at all times before God and the world. Therefore even if I should now be vexed with him, he nevertheless neither could nor desired to speak otherwise of me than as of one with a pious and sanctified heart. This I was to expect of him as though Christ Jesus Himself were saying it to me directly. He would damn himself and be the worst scoundrel and scamp if ever in my lifetime I should find and experience him to be otherwise. He spent two whole hours in making me such mighty assurances; I accepted them in simple faith, actually considering everything that Master Matthesius had faithfully reported to be nothing but a fabrication. However, Dr. Jakob still did not let up but kept pressing me that I should reveal to him who had reported such things to me. When I again and again refused to do so and instead urged and begged that he should let the matter rest and not insist upon knowing more, that eventually everything would be disclosed, he said: "Dear sir and brother, I do not wish to hold you in any suspicion; therefore I say that unless you indicate to me from whom you heard these things, I will consider you yourself to have fabricated them in order to have a reason for breaking off our relationship." In this manner he continued to insist on knowing until finally after frequent refusals and much hesitation I answered: "Okay. In order that you might see that I wish to deal with you openly, honestly, and as a brother, without any deception, I am in no way afraid to name to you my informant, namely, my house-companion, Master Matthesius." With that Dr. Jakob leveled a curse at Master Matthesius the like of which cannot be described. He also spoke most disparagingly of Master Lysthenius, urging and warning me to avoid them as being both my and his worst enemies. Once again, standing at the foot of the cross and calling upon Christ, he promised me his deepest loyalty and devotion and gave me his hand on it. Accordingly I again began sincerely to trust him and let him read any correspondence that I received concerning him, in order that he might sense my genuine integrity.

In June of 1577 Dr. Jakob had dealings with Master Lysthenius in which he said the worst about me and convinced him that he should urge his son-in-law, Master Matthesius, to compose a document directed against me in which he would report whatever he had heard me say about Dr. Jakob. Master Matthesius did in fact write such a document, and on the 14th of June Dr. Jakob presented it to me while in his own home, since he had returned to Leipzig from court. He maintained that Master Lysthenius had forwarded the document to him against his will, in order that I might read and respond to it as to how he was to take it. As I was deeply moved, I composed an answer within an hour and a half in which I expressed my innermost feelings. This I gave to Dr. Jakob with the condition that he give it to Master Lysthenius to read and then immediately tear it to bits and throw it in the fire. He promised to do this, but he did not keep his promise. In this way he undertook, as he knows how, in a most vicious manner to set Master Lysthenius, myself, and Master Matthesius against each other. Since I have no reason to be ashamed of my conduct, I wished to bring the matter to the attention of our gracious lord and to request a hearing, but Dr. Jakob repeatedly spoke and worked to prevent it. He verbally attacked Master Lysthenius for having permitted his son-in-law to compose the document and said: "There you see what kind of a fellow he is and how he feels about you!"

In July of 1577, on the 22nd, he said in a great burst of anger while in the upstairs room of his home (apparently he had just received a communication from my gracious lord, the point of which is unknown to me): "I don't care what the elector thinks; I haven't toadied to him in the past, and it's all the same to me whether he considers me favorably or unfavorably. What should one make of his vacillation, especially the fact that he doesn't dismiss Mirus? I'll let him know yet in clear German and rub it under his nose: 'If you dismiss him, great! If you don't, just let me know that you no longer need me.' The elector will soon enough discover his dilemma, for he himself has told me more than once that he does not have one single loyal adviser and knows no one whom he can trust. And when I have once again returned home, I'll let it be known that never have I become acquainted with more untruthful, disloyal, faithless people at a court or anywhere else on the face of the earth than in Meissen. All this I will report to my own pious lord. And I'll not advise the elector that I will for the rest of my life permit a few people to seethe in these facts." At that point I asked him please to refrain from and to spare me such talk. But he only became more unrestrained. And when he immediately blamed me that I would write Chemnitz what I had just heard, I answered him: I see repeatedly that he and I would not agree and that what he said against my lord and the charges with which he did me violence and injustice were unbearable and neither to be excused nor covered up. Accordingly I wished right now by hand and mouth to discontinue all fellowship and friendship, never to have anything to do with him again, and thus to rid myself of him. With that he offered me his hand. As I, however, was going down the steps, he runs after me, shouting: "My brother, not like this! Take me back, receive my apologies, and put the best construction on it. Say: 'His temper got the best of him.' Consider the offense which would result from our disagreement."

August. On the 1st of August at Weissensee, while at the hostel, he came down on me heavily again, this time in reference to the consistories, which he was eager to dismantle and disband. On Aug. 16 at Koburg, he said: "If I were now to write the elector, it would be pointless, for I can imagine you writing a different version; therefore we must part and go our separate ways. We do not have the same spirit." However, after I left him and went to bed, he soon followed; as he opened the bedroom door, he shouted: "You hopeless rogue, you worthless rascal, you arch knave, you barbarous thief, etc." I simply held my peace, and the next morning he said he had meant his attendant Martinus. I had to leave it at that. Later he provoked such a scene while at dinner with Dr. Maximilian Moerlin that I rose and left the table. But Dr. Maximilian wept bitterly and lamented the wretched state of the churches, which would become even worse at the hands of Dr. Jakob. At Gotha, Weimar, Altenburg, and Wurzen, he conducted himself toward me in such a way that I often thought he was about to beat me. Whatever his amanuensis had to endure from him, this I too had to suffer and then some.

On the 11th of September Dr. Jakob received a communication wherein my gracious lord expressed the desire that he should write a response to several points which the landgrave had brought to his attention. Dr. Jakob became so angry about this that on Sept. 14, while at Britsch in the home of Hans Loeser, hereditary marshal in the chamber, as he was going to bed he began all over again: "Why does the elector torture me with the landgrave's senseless babblings? After all, I am not the elector's servant. If only he would let me in peace. I've never received help from him in the past, and I don't need it now. I can get along very well without him and his inconstancy." Then he asked me to write His Electoral Grace and to commend him on the job he had been doing, as

I had gotten to know it on my trips (a job someone else could have done as well and with more forbearance). I answered him that this could still be done once the entire circuit had been completed. With this he was satisfied and silenced. On the 17th of September in Berlin while at luncheon and in the presence of some of the foremost advisers of the Elector of Brandenburg, he spoke disparagingly of the consistory. He said that a theologian should not be concerned about marriage problems; if, however, a theologian had spent two years with the consistory in working through questions dealing with marriage, he should spend the third year dealing with a good brothel-keeper. Since I politely refused to be partner to such frivolous language and briefly referred to Dr. Luther's opinion on the matter, he became very irritated with me. I arose from the table and escaped from his presence. However, for three entire days thereafter he did not wish to speak a word to me. On Sept. 27 he wished to make the trip to Gluecksburg to see my gracious lord and to take me along in order to make our report. But since I hesitated to make a joint report with him, I excused myself by referring also to the Festival of St. Michael, for which I should be present with my congregation, and so I asked him to give his own report. This upset him greatly and he went his way in anger. I, however, wished to save my report for an occasion when the elector might hear me for myself.

On the 6th of December, 1577, he got into a violent argument with me about the communication of attributes and mockingly charged me that Chemnitz and I still did not understand exactly what it was all about. This applied also to old Dr. Musculus, whom he said he wished to persuade that there was a cow by the name of Barthel, but that he would have to deal cautiously with him. Among other things he said: "Do you think I am satisfied with the so-called *Formula concordiae*? Chemnitz dragged the 'three classes of the communication of Christ's attributes' into it. This, however, was contrary to my wishes, and my own opinion is not that expressed therein." Upon which I said: "Lord God, what is the meaning of this? On the entire trip you have been repeatedly saying there is not a letter in that book which does not test out as pure gold and if you should have taught or written anything contrary thereto or should you do so in the future, that ought to be condemned and damned for all eternity!" At that he became alarmed and answered that he wished to discuss the matter with Chemnitz in my presence.

On March 13, 1578, at Tangermuende on the Elbe I was asked by the theologians just then assembled there to compose a statement that was thereupon to be submitted to the electors both of Saxony and of Brandenburg. Shortly thereafter Dr. Jakob indicated that the Elector of Saxony said to him: "Dr. Jakob, it is apparent to me that you did not compose this statement. It is not done in your style, and I would like to see it changed." Consequently he had to explain why he himself had not written it. Dr. Chemnitz can testify to the spiteful controversy which during the same month he provoked with me at

November. The story of the synod at Dresden is one that calls for mercy. God preserve me and all those who love peace from such a synod in which Dr. Jakob simply rebukes people, whether living or dead, whether prominent or not, including even members of our own dear government. I don't know one person throughout this land (with one single exception) of whom he speaks well, and yet he would have everyone believe, even adding an oath, that his intentions are just and noble while they are nothing of the sort. His own virtues are: wantonness, Langensalza. It was so bad I had to flee his presence until on the following day he had once again gained his composure.

During the month of April while he lay sick at Dresden he continually complained and insisted that he had been given poison. It had supposedly been given him at court or at the home of the chamberlain or that of Endres Kragen. He would not let anyone persuade him otherwise.

In August at Herzberg Master Amlungus, pastor at Zerbst, accused Dr. Jakob of having said that Satan himself had concocted the doctrine of the communication of attributes, whether spoken of abstractly or concretely. Dr. Jakob very vigorously denied this. However, he had frequently mentioned this to me, and this is his pattern: What he says today, he denies tomorrow. Also during August when I was carrying on a disputation at Leipzig and Dr. Simonius publicly made the statement that the physical body of Christ was everywhere present, including also in the toilet, a statement which shocked everyone, and when I refused to endure such blasphemous language, Dr. Jakob took the part of Simonius and wished particularly to postpone and forbid the repetition of my disputation (which he also did) until his return, at which time he himself wanted to give a teaching on the ubiquity. But because I realized how this would only cause a new stumbling block, especially since one could already hear blasphemous discussions among the parishioners as to how the body of Christ was present in a stone, dung, and cheese as well as in the Sacrament, as the Italian doctor had maintained, and because Dr. Jakob had also given me to understand that he wished to settle the matter by making a distinction between the following expressions: (1) the body of Christ is present in dung, and (2) the body of Christ is trapped in dung (the first he would consider true, the second, however, false), I continued with my disputation and paid no heed to Dr. Jakob's prohibition but silenced everyone and forbade the discussion of all the new offensive theses of Dr. Simonius and Dr. Jakob by simply cutting it off.

In October at Schmalkalden he repeated his oft-expressed opinion that he had no intention of condoning the elector should he retain the services of Mirus and should he not reject Thurneysen. He wondered what he should have to do with a ruler who marched under the banner of Satan. And when I said to him that such a charge still had to be proved, he became very angry and lumped everyone who had even received correspondence from Thurneysen under Satan's banner.

ambition, greed, contradictoriness, defiance, vengefulness, hyprocrisy, flattery, disloyalty, and contempt of everyone else.

During the month of December 1578 Dr. Jakob informed me through Dr. Polycarp, since he had noticed that I was disassociating myself from him and was probably letting it be known how I felt about him (as though he were not doing the same thing about me), that he wished hereby to pledge and promise me that in the future he intended to make no more reference to me, whether it be among prominent people or otherwise and whether it be in reference to good things or bad. For this offer I had my thanks extended to him and bade him keep his promise and do as he had said he would.

On Jan. 15, 1579, I sent my correspondence to the elector. On the 19th of January I met Dr. Jakob as he was walking toward me at the town hall in Jueterbog. He said: "Well, slit my throat from one end to the other!" Then he turned to Chemnitz and said: "See, Chemnitz, how people treat me! This fellow spreads all kinds of rumors about me, and once we were brothers and colleagues!" To which I answered that he should hold his tongue, for the situation was altogether other than he had described it. At that he wanted to faint and die, particularly when I told him that nothing was doing him harm other than his own evil tongue. The argument was ended by the intervention of the other theologians. Dr. Chemnitz, however, repeated his previous opinion and said: "If I should speak my conscience, it would be best if Dr. Jakob were again to be sent home. Otherwise we will never have tranquility and unity. The man accomplishes nothing of value and gets in the way more than he helps, for he scares people off from us." On Jan. 25 he gave us his blessing and asked to be pardoned if he had offended anyone with his words. How he kept his apology, however, his conscience knows best of all.

He seldom prays. He very seldom communes. He gives no alms to the poor. He rarely speaks the truth. He frequently maligns. He sows strife among brethren. He desires vengeance more than anything; he is contemptuous of others; he wants all the credit for himself; he grieves the Holy Spirit in many faithful believers. As a wolf-fish is among fish, so is he among men of his own rank; he heeds the warnings of none unless he is forced to do so by the authority of his superiors; what he says one minute, he denies the next; he takes oaths rashly and calls God to witness falsely; he deceives all who do not know him; he is meddlesome, a busybody, an exulter in other men's misfortunes. He speaks well of no prince but his own. He is a fickle blabbermouth, spiteful, treacherous. Be gracious, O God, convert the man or force him as judge![6]

For the following reasons I wish to keep this document in my possession: (1) Dr. Jakob apologized to me for much of the above in confession; (2) it would provoke a great deal of offense; (3) my gracious lord would be upset by it; (4) Dr. Jakob will not admit anything even if it is proved, but as soon as he recognizes himself to be convicted, he will deny everything by giving great assurances sealed with an oath; (5) I wish to commend it all into God's hands. But if Dr. Jakob should wish to injure the church even further and to deform this land or to further impose his poison upon me and swear falsely against me, as he has been accustomed to do in the past, then I wish to or (should I die) my wife shall have these brief notes delivered in the name of God to my gracious lord. And I humbly ask that when His Electoral Grace has read it, he destroy it in fire that any further offense in Christendom might be avoided. Written by my own hand, Jan. 29, 1579.

Footnotes to Appendix

1. Translated from the text published under the following title: Ein Christliche Predig Uber das Evangelium auff den XXIIII. Sontag nach Trinitatis/Mattheiam 24. Von vielen und mancherley verfuerungen in der Kirchen Gottes / vor dem Juengsten tage. Wie die eingefallene streitige Artikel unter den Lehrern Augsp. Confession dieser Landen Christlich verglichen / Und ein jeder Leye / aus seinem Heiligen einfeltigen Kinder Catechismo gruendtlich dieselbe urtheilen / und vor aller verfuerung moege bewaret werden. Gehalten zu Weymar den 24. Novemb. Anno 1577. Durch Jacobum Andreae D.

[A Christian sermon on the Gospel for the Twenty-Fourth Sunday After Trinity, Matthew 24: Regarding many and various deviations in the church of God before the final judgment and how the articles attacked and disputed among the teachers in these territories committed to the Augsburg Confession were settled in a Christian fashion. Also how each lay-person might thoroughly evaluate the same on the basis of his holy and simple Children's Catechism and thus be protected against every deviation. Given at Weimar on Nov. 24, 1577, by Dr. Jakob Andreae.]

2. Translated from the text published in Eduard Bodemann's article entitled "Herzog Julius von Braunschweig als deutscher Reichsfuerst, 1568—1589" in *Zeitschrift des historischen Vereins fuer Niedersachsen*, Jg. 1887 (Nr. 49, Bd. XX), pp. 36—40.

3. Translated from the text published under the following title: Historia Der Augspurgische Confession: Wie sie erstlich berahtschlagt / verfasset / und Keiser Carolo V, ubergeben ist / sampt andern Religions Handlungen / so sich dabey auff dem Reichstag zu Augspurg / Anno MDXXX zugetragen: Durch D. Davidem Chytraeum erstlich zusammen geordnet / vermehret / und nun endtlich widerumb durchsehen. Gedruckt zu Franckfurt am Mayn. MDLXXX.

[History of the Augsburg Confession: How it was originally deliberated, composed, and submitted to Emperor Charles V. Also other theological deliberations as occurred at the Diet of Augsburg in 1530. Originally prepared, published, and now finally revised by Dr. David Chytraeus. Published at Frankfurt/Main, 1580.]

4. Translated from the text published by H. Schnell in *Neue kirchliche Zeitschrift*, XI (1900), 175—80, under the title: "Ein Zeugnis des Rostocker Theologen David Chytraeus ueber den Abendmahlstreit." This "testimony" was given by Chytraeus to Duke Ulrich (1555—1603) of Mecklenburg at the latter's request.

5. Translated from the text of the diary as published in the archival studies of Th. Pressel entitled: "Die fuenf Jahre des Dr. Jakob Andreae in Chursachsen," *Jahrbuecher fuer Deutsche Theologie*, 22 (1877), 239—49.

6. This paragraph Selnecker wrote in a mixture of Latin and Greek.

Selected Bibliography

Encyclopedias

The Encyclopedia of the Lutheran Church. J. Bodensieck, ed. Minneapolis: Augsburg, 1965.

    Pertinent entries consulted:

        Andreae, Jakob, by Arthur C. Piepkorn

        Chemnitz, Martin, by Arthur C. Piepkorn

        Chytraeus, David, by Arthur C. Piepkorn

        Selnecker, Nikolaus, by Walter E. Buszin

        Formula of Concord, by Wilhelm Maurer, Tr.

Realencyklopaedie fuer protestantische Theologie und Kirche. Third Edition. Hauck-Herzog, eds. Leipzig: J. C. Hinrichs'sche Buchhandlung, 1896-1913.

    Pertinent entries consulted:

        Andreae, Jakob, by Wagenmann/Kolde

        Chemnitz, Martin, by Schmid/Kunze

        Chytraeus, David, by Georg Loesche

        Selnecker, Nikolaus, by Wagenmann/Dibelius

        Konkordienformel, by F. Frank

Die Religion in Geschichte und Gegenwart. Third Edition. Kurt Galling, ed. Tuebingen: J. C. B. Mohr, 1957-1965.

    Pertinent entries consulted:

        Andreae, Jakob, by R. Mueller-Streisand

        Chemnitz, Martin, by F. Lau

        Chytraeus, David, by G. Loesche/H. Liebing

        Selnecker, Nikolaus, by W. Jannasch

        Konkordienformel, by Ernst Wolf.

Lutheran Confessions

Die Bekenntnisschriften der evangelisch-lutherischen Kirche. Third Revised Edition. Goettingen: Vandenhoeck und Ruprecht, 1956.

The Book of Concord. T. G. Tappert, ed. Philadelphia: Muhlenberg, 1959.

Triglot Concordia. The Symbolical Books of the Evangelical Lutheran Church (German, Latin, English). F. Bente, ed., with general introduction. St. Louis: Concordia, 1921.

Books and Articles

Barton, Peter F. *Um Luthers Erbe: Studien und Texte zur Spaetreformation—Tilemann Heshusius (1527—1559)*. Witten: Luther-Verlag, 1972.

Bente, G. Friedrich. *Historical Introductions to the Book of Concord*. St. Louis: Concordia Publishing House, 1921/1965.

Bodemann, Eduard. "Herzog Julius von Braunschweig als deutscher Reichsfuerst, 1568—1589," *Zeitschrift des historischen Vereins fuer Niedersachsen*, Jg. 1887, 1—92.

Chemnitz, Martin. *The Two Natures in Christ*, trans. J. A. O. Preus. St. Louis: Concordia Publishing House, 1971.

Dibelius, Franz. "Zur Geschichte und Charakteristik Nikolaus Selneckers," *Beitraege zur saechsischen Kirchengeschichte*, IV (1888), 1—20.

Elert, Werner. *The Structure of Lutheranism*, trans. Walter Hansen. St. Louis: Concordia Publishing House, 1962.

Fittbogen, Chr. Moritz. *Jacob Andreae, der Verfasser des Concordienbuches: Sein Leben und seine theologische Bedeutung*. Leipzig: Hermann Risel, 1881.

Gensichen, Hans-Werner. *We Condemn: How Luther and 16th-Century Lutheranism Condemned False Doctrine*, trans. Herbert J. A. Bouman. St. Louis: Concordia Publishing House, 1967.

Gerrish, B. A. "John Calvin on Luther," *Interpreters of Luther*, ed. Jaroslav Pelikan. Philadelphia: Fortress Press, 1968. Pp. 67—96.

Graebner, August L., trans. "An Autobiography of Martin Kemnitz," *Theological Quarterly*, III/4 (October 1899), 472—87.

Gruemmer, Richard. *Andreas Musculus: Sein Leben und seine Werke*. Eisenach: H. Kahle, 1912.

Guersching, Heinrich. "Jakob Andreae und seine Zeit," *Blaetter fuer Wuerttembergische Kirchengeschichte*, LIV (1954), 123—56.

Hachfeld, Hermann. *Martin Chemnitz nach seinem Leben und Wirken, insbesondere nach seinem Verhaeltnisse zum Tridentinum*. Leipzig: Breitkopf und Haertel, 1867.

Hermelink, Heinrich. *Geschichte der evangelischen Kirche in Wuerttemberg von der Reformation bis zur Gegenwart*. Stuttgart and Tuebingen: Rainer Wunderlich Verlag, 1949.

Johannsen, J. C. G. "Jakob Andreae's concordistische Thaetigkeit," *Zeitschrift fuer die historische Theologie*, XXIII (1853), Nr. 3. Pp. 344—415.

Klatt, Detloff. *David Chytraeus als Geschichtslehrer und Geschichtschreiber*. Rostock: Adlers Erben, 1908.

Klaus, Bernhard. *Veit Dietrich: Amanuenses D. Martin Luthers und Prediger an St. Sebald in Nuernberg*. Nuernberg: Selbstverlag des Vereins fuer bayerische Kirchengeschichte, 1958.

Klug, E. F. *From Luther to Chemnitz on Scripture and the Word.* Grand Rapids: Eerdmans, 1971.

Koch, Eduard Emil. *Geschichte des Kirchenlieds und Kirchengesangs der christlichen, insbesondere der deutschen evangelischen Kirche,* I, "Selneccer." Stuttgart: Druck und Verlag der Chr. Belser'schen Buchhandlung, 1852. Pp. 160— 68.

Kolb, Robert. "Six Christian Sermons on the Way to Lutheran Unity," *Concordia Theological Monthly,* XLIV (1973), 261—74.

Koldewey, Friedrich. "Neun bisher nicht gedruckte Briefe Melanchthons ueber und an Martin Kemnitz," *Zeitschrift fuer die historische Theologie,* XLII (1872), 3—23.

Maurer, Wilhelm. *Der junge Melanchthon zwischen Humanismus und Reformation.* 2 vols. Goettingen: Vandenhoeck und Ruprecht, 1967/1969.

Montgomery, John Warwick. *Chytraeus on Sacrifice: A Reformation Treatise in Biblical Theology.* St. Louis: Concordia Publishing House, 1962.

Mueller-Streisand, Rosemarie. "Theologie und Kirchenpolitik bei Jakob Andreae bis zum Jahr 1568," *Blaetter fuer wuerttembergische Kirchengeschichte,* LX/LXI (1960/1961), 224—395.

Mumm, Reinhard. *Die Polemik des Martin Chemnitz gegen das Konzil von Trient.* Leipzig: A. Deichert, 1905.

Noth, Gottfried. *Grundzuege der Theologie des Martin Chemnitz.* Erlangen: Gutenberg, 1930.

Piepkorn, Arthur Carl. "Martin Chemnitz' Views on Trent: The Genesis and Genius of the *Examen Concilii Tridentini,*" *Concordia Theological Monthly,* XXXVII (January 1966), 5—37.

Polack, W. G. *The Handbook to the Lutheran Hymnal.* St. Louis: Concordia Publishing House, 1942.

Pressel, Theodor. "Die fuenf Jahre des Dr. Jakob Andreae in Chursachsen," *Jahrbuecher fuer Deutsche Theologie,* XXII (1877), 1—64; 207—64.

——————. "Martin Chemnitz." *Leben und ausgewaehlte Schriften der Vaeter und Begruender der lutherischen Kirche, VIII. Teil.* Elberfeld: R. L. Friderichs, 1862.

——————. "David Chytraeus." *Leben und ausgewaehlte Schriften der Vaeter und Begruender der lutherischen Kirche, VIII. Teil.* Elberfeld: R. L. Friderichs, 1862.

——————. "Zwei Actenstuecke zur Genesis der Concordienformel," *Jahrbuecher fuer Deutsche Theologie,* XI (1866), 640—743.

Preus, Herman A., and Edmund Smits, eds. *The Doctrine of Man in Classical Lutheran Theology.* Minneapolis: Augsburg Publishing House, 1962.

Preus, Robert D. *The Theology of Post-Reformation Lutheranism: A Study of Theological Prolegomena.* St. Louis: Concordia Publishing House, 1970.

Rogness, Michael. *Philip Melanchthon: Reformer Without Honor.* Minneapolis: Augsburg, 1969.

Sasse, Hermann. *This Is My Body: Luther's Contention for the Real Presence in the Sacrament of the Altar.* Minneapolis: Augsburg, 1959.

Schlink, Edmund. *Theology of the Lutheran Confessions*, trans. Paul F. Koehneke and Herbert J. A. Bouman. Philadelphia: Muhlenberg Press, 1961.

Schmauk, T. E., and C. T. Benze. *The Confessional Principle and the Confessions of the Lutheran Church.* Philadelphia: General Council Publication Board, 1911.

Winkler, Eberhard. "Die Leichenpredigt im deutschen Lutherthum bis Spener," *Forschungen zur Geschichte und Lehre des Protestantismus*, ed. Ernst Wolf, Series 10, Vol. XXXIV. Muenchen: Chr. Kaiser, 1967. S. v. "Nikolaus Selnecker." Pp. 90—103.